Canada Law Book ⌐ᵤₚ

Mediating Employment Disputes

Second Edition

Barry Kuretzky · Jennifer MacKenzie

CANADA LAW BOOK®

A cataloguing record for this publication is available from Library and Archives Canada.

ISBN 978-0-88804-667-3

Printed in Canada by Thomson Reuters.

TELL US HOW WE'RE DOING
Scan the QR code to the right with your smartphone to send your comments regarding our products and services.
Free QR Code Readers are available from your mobile device app store.
You can also email us at carswell.feedback@thomsonreuters.com

CARSWELL, A DIVISION OF THOMSON REUTERS CANADA LIMITED

One Corporate Plaza	**Customer Relations**
2075 Kennedy Road	Toronto 1-416-609-3800
Toronto, Ontario	Elsewhere in Canada/U.S. 1-800-387-5164
M1T 3V4	Fax 1-416-298-5082
www.carswell.com	E-mail www.carswell.com/email

PREFACE

It is trite to say that employment law involves very sensitive issues. Anyone who practises in the area of employment law realizes that an employment law dispute is about much more than just money. For an employee, it is often also about emotions, respect, self-esteem, family issues and a sense of fairness. For an employer, it may be about running an effective business, employee morale and equity, among many other things. Since there may be a lot at stake for both parties to an employment law dispute, there is often a driving desire to find a suitable solution that is efficient from a time and cost perspective, as well as one that is viewed by both parties as fair and equitable.

In many employment law disputes, mediation is the best tool for achieving these goals. When we wrote the first edition of this book in 2001, mediation in employment law in Canada was still in the developing stages. Today, it is a key part of employment litigation. Recently, there have been further developments in "workplace mediations" and it is in this area that we will likely see even wider application in the future. Although it is not extensively used by employment lawyers, in our view, there is certainly still room for further development and advancement.

In this book, we have endeavoured to provide lawyers with a practical guide to the mediation process as it pertains to the practice of employment law. It is our view that preparing your client, and your client's case, for a mediation, is like preparing for a quasi-judicial process. We have included what we hope will be useful precedents, checklists and tips. Certain portions of the book may be extracted by counsel to be shared with clients. Although some of the information we have presented may appear obvious to experienced counsel, certain aspects of the process are often overlooked. Even counsel who has been involved in many employment law mediations may find this book useful as it should allow them to step back and explore the practical side of mediation and provide them with a framework within which to work. We have also developed more detailed information on "workplace mediations" to assist practitioners and clients who are working towards resolving internal workplace disputes.

Toronto, Ontario   Barry Kuretzky
March 2013   Jennifer MacKenzie

iii

TABLE OF CONTENTS

TABLE OF CONTENTS

Chapter 1

MEDIATION IN THE EMPLOYMENT LAW SETTING

1. INTRODUCTION

Mediation is the most common form of alternative dispute resolution. It is used widely in many areas of the law. Mediation provides an alternative dispute resolution mechanism to parties who wish to resolve their own dispute as well as avoid further conflict and expensive litigation. Mediation involves the assistance of a neutral third party mediator who assists the parties to resolve their differences and reach a consensual resolution by facilitating discussion. The defining feature of mediation is its flexibility. Disputing parties can overcome barriers to communication by a flexible mediation process in which the parties retain ownership and control. Over the past decade, the use of mediation as a means of resolving employment law disputes has become increasingly common and it is an area of the law where mediation has quite a high success rate.

This chapter will provide a general overview of the concept of mediation as it applies to employment law disputes. We will outline the four models of mediation that have the widest application to employment law. We will also provide a general overview of the most commonly encountered legal issues in employment law and highlight the application of mediation to resolving these issues. We will also compare employment law mediation to other legal disciplines, canvass the numerous benefits of mediation and analyze the application of court-mandated mediation versus voluntary mediation.

2. MODELS OF MEDIATION

Mediation practices tend to vary depending on a number of circumstances, including the personal characteristics of the parties, the mediator, the nature of the dispute and the desired outcome. The

1

following four models provide a framework for the mediation process as they apply to employment law. However, it is important to note that a mediation will rarely follow just one model. The flexibility inherent in mediation allows the parties to adopt aspects from a variety of models in order to individualize the process to meet their particular needs and interests.

(a) Transformative Mediation

The goal of transformative mediation is the reconciliation of the parties to a dispute. This type of therapeutic mediation aims to improve the parties' communication and relationship by addressing the causes of their problem(s). The parties define the dispute based on behavioural, emotional, communication and relationship factors. Mediators are sensitive to the psychological factors driving the conflict and encourage the parties to listen and communicate with the other party to address the problems underlying the relationship. In fact, in a transformative mediation, relationship issues are addressed before there is any decision-making with respect to the dispute. The process is designed to empower the parties by encouraging them to take ownership of the process as well as the outcome.

A noted strength of transformative mediation is that parties often "resolve" rather than "settle" their dispute. However, there are weaknesses to this type of mediation which include the chance that the mediation may be prolonged without a solution and further, that the mediators are at risk of confusing counselling with their mediation roles. In fact, the philosophy behind transformative mediation is that mediation can change how people behave, not only towards their opponent but in their day-to-day lives and attitudes. Accordingly, the goal of resolution of the dispute may be overlooked. Transformative mediation is appropriate for cases where there may be a continuing relationship between the parties or where contracts are unexpectedly terminated, such as in an employment, family or business relationship.

(b) Facilitative Mediation

Facilitative mediation is interest-based. Through facilitative mediation, the parties are encouraged to avoid their strict legal positions and focus on negotiating a mutual resolution based on their underlying interests, goals and needs. In facilitative mediation, the mediator typically has expertise in the mediation procedure but does not necessarily have

2

knowledge of the subject-matter of the dispute. The mediator facilitates a problem-solving process by encouraging purposeful and meaningful discussion between the parties. The mediator may ask questions to identify the interests and real issues of disagreement. The mediator will help the parties identify and evaluate options for resolution and settlement. The mediator's level of intervention may be limited since it is the responsibility of the parties to produce creative options based on their interests. However, the mediator assists the parties in applying objective criteria which allows them to choose from the possible options. The mediator will not suggest solutions but will bring forward the ideas.

The advantage of facilitative mediation is that the process is controlled by the parties, which allows them to maximize negotiation options. However, there are drawbacks which include the requirement that the parties be prepared to settle the dispute and actively participate in the process. In addition, there is a possibility that the mediation will be lengthy and a resolution may not be reached. Facilitative mediation is commonly used for mediating personal injury, municipal, neighbourhood and business disputes. As will be outlined later in this book, certain features of this model, in particular the creative solutions that it permits, have broad application for employment law disputes.

(c)   Settlement Mediation

Settlement mediation is also referred to as "results-based mediation" or "compromise mediation". The purpose of this model of mediation is for the parties to define the problem and to gradually negotiate towards a compromise based on their positional demands. In settlement mediation, the role of the mediator is limited. In this form of mediation, the mediator is typically a high-status individual, such as a lawyer or retired judge who does not necessarily have skills or training in the mediation process. He or she will determine the parties' "bottom lines" and employ various persuasive techniques to move the parties away from their positions and towards a mutual compromise.

The advantages of settlement mediation are that the process can be easily understood by the parties, the mediation can be easily executed, and little advance preparation is required. However, settlement mediation is limited in some respects in that it often disregards the parties' interests and needs and consequently, a final resolution may be difficult to achieve. Areas of practice in which settlement mediation is often used include commercial law and personal injury disputes. In the area of employment law, a form of settlement mediation often takes place by judges at

3

pretrial/settlement conferences. It can be particularly useful in employment law where liability is not an issue but the parties are in disagreement
with respect to the amount of and characterization of damages that
should be paid. In fact, many employment law disputes would be well
served by a settlement mediation. Where the issues are straight-forward, a
settlement often results from the parties reaching a mutually satisfying
compromise. However, where the issues in dispute are more complex or
sensitive (which is sometimes the case in employment law disputes) this
form of mediation may not be appropriate.

(d) Evaluative Mediation

Evaluative mediation is rights-based mediation that is based on an
advisory framework and is sometimes referred to as "non-binding
arbitration". Through this model of mediation, the parties attempt to
reach a settlement based on legal rules and the expected range of what a
court would order based on the facts and circumstances of the case. The
dispute is defined in terms of the parties' legal rights, industry standards
or community norms. In an evaluative mediation, mediators have high
interventionist roles and usually possess professional and substantive
expertise in the area of the dispute. Generally speaking, the mediator will
be a neutral third party who provides an independent assessment on the
legal and equitable rights of the parties as well as the likely outcome of
the case if a settlement is not reached by mediation. The mediator advises
the parties, provides further information and persuades the parties to
reach an outcome. In this model of mediation, the mediator is more likely
to give an opinion, recommend options and advise on the court's likely
outcome. Rights-based mediation is appropriate when one party believes
that the other party has an unrealistic perception of the outcome or the
parties believe that the mediator's opinions will be influential on one or
both of the parties. It may also be useful if counsel believes that his or her
client has an unreasonable assessment of the case and would benefit from
a "reality check".

Advantages of evaluative mediation are that the mediator brings
substantive expertise to the process and the outcomes are typically within
the range of court decisions dealing with similar disputes. However,
disadvantages include that the parties themselves are less involved in the
process, the parties' feelings are generally unimportant, and the mediator
is at risk of blurring the distinction between mediation and arbitration.
Evaluative mediation is commonly used in anti-discrimination trade
practices, personal injury and commercial disputes. Certain aspects of

evaluative mediation have application to employment law disputes, particularly where liability is an issue in the matter. It can also have application to employment matters that involve the interpretation of a contract or the application of restrictive covenants such as non-competition and non-solicitation clauses.

3. GENERAL OVERVIEW OF LEGAL ISSUES IN AN EMPLOYMENT LAW MATTER

It is important to understand the scope of employment law in order to effectively apply the mediation process to an employment law dispute. As with most legal matters, each employment law matter involves a unique set of circumstances. Typically, there will be a number of legal issues of varying significance and complexity. Although some employment law matters will be confined to one or two fairly straightforward issues, others may involve an array of complicated and interrelated legal issues. By their nature, certain employment law matters lend themselves easily to the mediation process and will fit easily within the confines of the mediation models set out above. However, mediation can be configured to suit almost any employment law matter when the willingness of the parties exists.

In most cases, at the time a lawyer is retained with respect to an employment law matter, the employment relationship in question has already been terminated. In cases of wrongful dismissal, the issues to be resolved between the parties may include a determination of whether cause exists for the termination and if not, a determination of what is the appropriate period of reasonable notice to be awarded to an employee. That is employment law at its most rudimentary level. In most cases, there will be an assortment of other issues with which to contend. As discussed below, there may be complex issues of compensation. The case may also involve substantial claims for other damages such as punitive damages, aggravated damages, damages for mental distress and damages for loss of reputation, particularly where the conduct of the employer has been perceived as unduly harsh. The matter may be especially sensitive where allegations of discrimination or harassment have been raised.

It should be noted that employment law matters do not only arise following the termination of an employment relationship. Disputes may arise between an employer and employee during the course of the employment relationship and may also arise between two or more employees of an employer. These sorts of disputes will be thoroughly addressed later in the book.

We will summarize the most common legal issues that may be encountered by counsel handling an employment law matter. Please note that this summary is not intended to be exhaustive of the legal issues that exist in employment law. The reader is advised to consult employment law resources for a more detailed analysis of the law.

(a) Just Cause

Where the employer asserts that there is just cause to terminate an employee's employment, the primary issue is whether just cause for termination in fact exists. Where just cause is found by a court, the employee will be entitled to no damages for reasonable notice. Where a court determines there is no just cause, an employee is likely to be awarded with reasonable notice, costs and possibly other damages. However, short of a court decision, it is often difficult for the parties to assess whether there is just cause for termination as few hard and fast rules exist. Although it is not possible to define precisely, just cause may include instances of theft from the employer, gross misuse of an expense account, fraud, gross insubordination or gross misconduct. Cause for termination may also exist where an employee's performance is inadequate despite an employer's unequivocal warnings to the employee and despite ample opportunity provided to the employee to improve performance. A large portion of "just cause" cases involve allegations of poor performance on the part of the terminated employee. Despite the number of reported cases that have addressed this issue and the frequency with which employers face this dilemma, it remains a somewhat grey area of employment law. That being said, a tough onus is typically placed on employers to demonstrate that just cause for termination exists. Most cases where cause is alleged will settle prior to the stage of trial. Normally, the behaviour in question must be quite reprehensible and contain elements of wilfulness to commit the act to constitute cause. The threshold for cause under employment standards legislation is typically even higher than it is under common law.

(b) Reasonable Notice

If there is no cause for termination, a key issue in a wrongful dismissal action involves a determination of what is the appropriate "period of reasonable notice" or "severance period" to which an employee is entitled. The determination of what constitutes reasonable notice is generally based on an assessment of factors such as the employee's age, length of service, position, compensation, marketability and whether the employee was induced from other employment to join the employer.[1] The purpose of reasonable notice is neither to act as a means of punishing the employer nor to provide the employee with a financial windfall. The rationale behind reasonable notice is to allow the employee a "reasonable period" to obtain new employment, based on a consideration of the relevant factors. Its intent is to bridge the gap between the date of termination and the commencement of new employment. The 1997 Supreme Court of Canada decision in *Wallace v. United Grain Growers Ltd.*[2] gave rise to the concept of "bad faith discharge" whereby an employer could be found to be liable for an extended notice period where the employer's conduct on termination was particularly harsh and unwarranted. However, the *Wallace*-style extended notice period was later replaced by compensatory bad faith damages based on actual damages suffered based on the Supreme Court's decision of *Keays v. Honda Canada Inc.*[3] In accordance with the *Honda* decision, damages for mental distress are available only if mental distress is beyond normal hurt feelings that arise from termination and was caused by the employer's bad faith conduct. Such damages are also only available to the extent that actual mental distress is proved.

(c) Mitigation

The issue of mitigation will arise in most actions for wrongful dismissal. The exception to the rule occurs where there exists a written employment contract between the parties that provides for the payment of severance on a termination without cause without the requirement of mitigation on the part of the employee. The principle of mitigation requires an employee to actively pursue other employment opportunities following the termination of employment. In theory, any income an employee earns during the "reasonable notice period" will be deducted from the award of reasonable notice. In the event an employee fails to make adequate efforts to mitigate damages, a judge has the authority to

---

[1] *Bardal v. Globe Mail Ltd.*, 1960 CarswellOnt 144, 24 D.L.R. (2d) 140, [1960] O.W.N. 253 (Ont. H.C.).

[2] *Wallace v. United Grain Growers Ltd.*, 1997 CarswellMan 455, 1997 CarswellMan 456, [1997] 3 S.C.R. 701, 3 C.B.R. (4th) 1, 36 C.C.E.L. (2d) 1, 152 D.L.R. (4th) 1, [1999] 4 W.W.R. 86, 97 C.L.L.C. 210-029, [1997] L.V.I. 2889-1, 123 Man. R. (2d) 1, 219 N.R. 161, 159 W.A.C. 1, [1997] S.C.J. No. 94 (S.C.C.).

[3] *Keays v. Honda Canada Inc.*, 2008 CarswellOnt 3743, 2008 CarswellOnt 3744, (sub nom. *Honda Canada Inc. v. Keays*) [2008] 2 S.C.R. 362, 294 D.L.R. (4th) 577, (sub nom. *Honda Canada Inc. v. Keays*) (S.C.C.).

deny or reduce the amount of reasonable notice to which an employee is entitled. During the course of a legal action and during the process of mediation, the employer and its lawyers are entitled to request evidence of the employee's mitigation efforts. These efforts may be scrutinized to assess the employee's efforts. However, typically, an employee's award of reasonable notice will only be reduced where the mitigation efforts were particularly flawed.

(d) Compensation

In many employment law disputes, especially those involving senior and executive employees, the employee's entitlement to various components of his or her compensation package may be disputed especially in relation to their application during the notice period. Sometimes there will exist issues of unpaid wages, including commission earnings and bonus payments for the period of employment preceding termination. Commonly there is a dispute with respect to what components of an employee's compensation should be included in calculating the *quantum* of reasonable notice. Not surprisingly, the employer often seeks to confine compensation to base salary. Where an employee was entitled to group insurance benefits during the period of employment, an issue may arise as to whether and how the employee should be compensated for the loss of these benefits for the reasonable notice period. There may also be a claim for pension accruals for the notice period. One of the most contentious points of compensation relates to bonus entitlement for the reasonable notice period. Disputes of this nature may include a determination of whether the bonus was purely discretionary and whether it formed an integral part of the employee's compensation. Some employers attempt to contract out of this entitlement even for the period of the year during which the employee worked. However, there has been case law that defines when this is deemed appropriate and when it is not. A decision of the Ontario Court of Appeal upheld the trial judge's decision in finding that an internal bonus plan requiring an employee to be employed when bonuses were paid could not operate to deprive an employee of bonus compensation in a without cause termination.[4] In that case, the court found that the employee's involuntary inability to comply with the conditions of the bonus plan that he be "actively employed" at the time that the award is paid could not be the employer's justification

---

[4]   *Schumacher v. Toronto Dominion Bank*, 1999 CarswellOnt 1523, 173 D.L.R. (4th) 577 (Ont. C.A.), leave to appeal refused (2000), 180 D.L.R. (4th) vi, [1999] S.C.C.A. No. 369 (S.C.C.).

for not paying the bonus. Where the bonus was promoted as an integral part of the employee's cash compensation, it would be inappropriate and unfair to the employee if he or she were deprived of the bonus by reason of the unilateral action of the employer.

Even more complex are issues involving stock options which have become a significant part of overall compensation for many employees. The legal issues usually revolve around what the appropriate exercise period of the options should be given the employee's termination of employment.

(e) Contract Issues

An increasing number of employment relationships are governed by a written employment agreement. Consequently, determination of contract disputes during both the course of an employment relationship and upon termination of employment is common. Often, such disputes revolve around the meaning and intent of provisions in the agreement. Many employment contracts contain language that is ambiguous and these contracts have been determined to be unenforceable as a result. One of the most contentious contractual matters concerns the meaning and application of a termination clause in an employment contract, including the definition of cause, the amount of severance, mitigation requirements and the structure of payments. Some contracts purport to limit any notice or severance to the statutory minimum requirements and if they do, a stumbling block is often a determination of whether valid consideration existed upon entering the contract.

(f) Restrictive Covenants

A significant issue that often arises between an employee and an employer upon the termination of an employment relationship relates to the post-employment obligations of the employee. Sometimes, disputes arise over the application and enforceability of non-competition and non-solicitation clauses contained in contracts signed by the employee prior to or during the course of the employment relationship. Other times, the employer may attempt to impose such restrictions upon the employee at the time of termination or during the negotiation of a severance package. This is often a complicated area of employment law and there are many factors that determine when a restrictive covenant is valid and when it is not. For instance, a restrictive covenant is more likely to be valid where the temporal length is reasonable (*i.e.*, three to six months rather than 12 to 24 months), the restricted geographic area is reasonable and the covenant does not purport to place an unreasonable restraint on trade.

(g)   Other Damages

Aside from reasonable notice for termination, there are other damages that may be claimed by an employee upon the termination of employment, depending on the circumstances of the case. Issues of entitlement to punitive damages, aggravated damages, damages for mental distress, damages for defamation and damages for loss of reputation may arise in the course of an employment law action. Although often claimed, damages of these kinds are not often awarded by courts and when awards are made, it is only in those cases where the behaviour of the employer was reprehensible and/or real damages can be proven.

(h)   Human Rights Considerations

The laws of every province of Canada and the federal jurisdiction strictly prohibit any form of discrimination in employment on several grounds including, but not limited to age, sex, marital/family status, race, ethnic origin, sexual orientation, disability and religion. Issues of alleged discrimination may arise with respect to the treatment of an employee during the course of an employment relationship or upon the termination of employment. This may be the subject of an internal complaint procedure or a formal human rights commission complaint. A legal action for "discrimination" may also be brought under the guise of other heads of damages, and in Ontario a breach of the *Human Rights Code*[5] can be pleaded in a statement of claim.

(i)   Disability

Issues of disability are becoming increasingly common in employment law matters and they are not without ambiguity. Where a disabled person is terminated from his or her employment or treated adversely during the course of an employment relationship, there may be human rights implications. Even where there is no issue of discrimination, issues often arise as to the interplay between periods of disability and periods of severance and whether these periods can run concurrently. The manner in which this issue is dealt with by the parties will often depend on the type

---

[5]   R.S.O. 1990, c. H.19.

of disability plan in existence. Another important issue that arises is whether to continue an employee's disability benefits following the termination of employment and the consequences of not doing so where an employee later falls ill. There are precedents that have found that an employer is on the hook for continuing disability income where the insurance has not been appropriately continued by the employer. These issues are typically very complex and sensitive and must be carefully addressed by the parties.

(j) Sexual or Other Forms of Harassment

Issues of harassment, whether of a sexual or other nature, are not uncommon during the course of an employment relationship but may also surface following the termination of employment. If it arises during the course of an employment relationship, the complaint must be taken seriously by the employer and a proper investigation must be conducted. Following this, the parties may attempt to resolve a dispute amicably amongst the accuser, accused and company, particularly where serious disciplinary measures are not warranted. Where the accused employee is disciplined or terminated, issues may arise as to the appropriateness of this action on the employer's part, and a legal action may be commenced by the accused employee for wrongful dismissal. In addition, over the past decade or so, anti-bullying, anti-harassment and anti-violence policies in the workplace have become standard and most employers would adopt a zero tolerance policy for this kind of behavior. Employers have had to learn how to address these issues and mediation is one manner in which they have been dealt with effectively.

4. APPLICATION OF MEDIATION TO AN EMPLOYMENT LAW MATTER

Mediation can be a very useful and effective tool for resolving employment law matters. Mediation started being used in employment law matters in the late 1980s and since then has become widely embraced. Some jurisdictions (including regions of Ontario) require mediation at an early stage in any litigation process (and this will be addressed more thoroughly later.) Mediation has clearly become an important mechanism to resolving employment law disputes.

There are three general scenarios for which mediation has application to employment law:

MEDIATING EMPLOYMENT DISPUTES

1. To resolve disputes between an employer and employee that arises upon termination of employment.
2. To resolve disputes between an employer and employee during the course of their employment relationship.
3. To resolve disputes internally between two or more employees of a company.

Mediation is most frequently used in resolving employment law disputes that fall within the first scenario. In cases of this nature, any number of issues, as outlined in the preceding section, may be on the table for negotiation between the parties. The model of mediation used and the style of the mediator may depend partly on the nature of and complexity of the issues. It will also depend on the needs, interests and goals of the parties. For disputes of this nature, any one of the four models of mediation or some combination thereof may be used, although transformative and facilitative mediation are probably the most commonly applied models. Where mediation is used to resolve a post-termination dispute, mediation can be used effectively at any stage of a legal proceeding — before an action is commenced, following the exchange of pleadings, after the production of documents and completion of examinations for discovery or just prior to trial. In Ontario, where mediation of employment matters is court mandated, the parties are required to attempt mediation at an early stage of the proceeding, after the exchange of pleadings.[6] Where mediation is used in resolving disputes in the second and third scenarios, since the parties are still governed by an employment relationship, it is unlikely that a legal action will have been commenced. Consequently, the mediation may adopt a different tone and style than that of a post-termination mediation. It would be quite common to utilize the transformative model because it allows behavioural, emotional, communication and relationship factors to be readily considered and the goal of the mediation will be reconciliation. Aspects of facilitative mediation may also be utilized.

At the time of first writing this book, formal mediation was not readily used by Canadian employers in dealing with internal workplace disputes. However, over the last decade, more employers have been embracing a form of mediation to resolve workplace disputes, which has commonly become known as "workplace mediation". Employers are becoming increasingly proactive in dealing with internal employment

---

[6] *Rules of Civil Procedure*, R.R.O. 1990, Reg. 194, Rule 24.1.

disputes through the use of workplace mediation. This will be discussed in greater detail in later chapters.

5. MEDIATION IN OTHER AREAS OF LAW

The nature of certain legal disputes lends themselves to some form of mediation better than others. In some areas of the practice of law, mediation is a well-established dispute resolution mechanism, and in other areas, it is less commonly used. In addition to employment law, mediation is commonly used in disputes occurring in the following areas of practice:

- Family Law
- Commercial/Business Law
- Construction Law
- Personal Injury Law
- Landlord and Tenant Law
- Environmental and Planning Law
- Medical Malpractice Law
- Health Law
- Estate Law
- Bankruptcy and Insolvency Law
- Neighbourhood and Community Law
- Education Law

Some of these areas, particularly family law, have developed a distinct body of guidelines, mediators and court-connected programs. There are virtually no guidelines and there are far fewer resources relating to mediation in employment law in Canada. There is, however, substantial authority in the United States. Although the models and processes used commonly in one area of the law may be largely ineffective in another area, they may still offer some helpful guidance. Over the years, employment law practitioners have borrowed certain aspects from these more established disciplines to create a much more defined use for employment law.

Mediation is useful in resolving commercial law disputes where a quick and amicable resolution is often required to preserve a business relationship. The same principle can certainly be applied where an employment relationship is sought to be preserved. However, in employment law cases, where the employer-employee relationship has ended, lawyers have looked to other areas of law such as family law where greater similarities in the characteristics of the parties and the nature of

13

the dispute may exist. For instance, power imbalances are often a major concern in matrimonial cases, especially where there is a history of domestic violence or financial dependency. In employment law mediation, the power imbalance between an employee with limited finances and resources against a highly equipped corporate employer are also relevant considerations. In these cases, the mediator may need to play a more active and controlling role in order to best facilitate a resolution between the parties. Where the power imbalance is severe, it may be determined that mediation is not a viable option, although provided that both parties are represented by counsel, this concern should be significantly lessened.[7] The flexibility inherent in mediation allows for all such concerns to be effectively addressed resulting in a unique process for each dispute. Family law has also embraced a collaborative law process in recent years, which is a concept that we feel may have wide application to employment law in the future. We will discuss this in more detail in Chapter 6.

6. BENEFITS OF MEDIATING EMPLOYMENT LAW MATTERS

There are many substantial benefits to be gained by the parties where mediation is embarked upon to resolve an employment law dispute.

A mediated resolution usually results in satisfaction by all parties since no settlement can be reached without the full consent, understanding, involvement and participation of the parties. The parties are given a sense of control over both the process of mediation and the result achieved. Where a legal action has been commenced or threatened, a mediated solution will avoid for both parties the inherent risks of trial. From our experience, although prepared to go all the way when necessary, most clients prefer a settlement over the unknowns of a trial as well as the tremendous preparation and stress that go along with it. Although mediation is not defined by "winners" and "losers", the parties may be immensely satisfied in knowing they have been instrumental in reaching an amicable settlement that they can both accept. In reality, with a mediated resolution, the parties sometimes feel more relief than satisfaction that they have resolved the matter.

In addition, through an employment law mediation, there are virtually no boundaries with respect to the nature of the resolution that

---

[7] See Chapter 8 "Special Issues in Mediating Employment Law Disputes", for a detailed analysis of power imbalances.

can be reached. The parties can use creativity (within the confines of the law) in structuring an appropriate settlement. They have the freedom to agree to items that would not be within the jurisdiction of a court to award. For instance, through mediation, an employee may be able to negotiate such terms as a positive letter of recommendation, a mutually acceptable reason for termination (sometimes characterizing a departure as a resignation/mutual parting rather than a termination) as well as outplacement counselling or educational course work. An employer may be able to negotiate a restrictive covenant that was not previously a term of the employment contract. On occasion, a terminated employee may agree to provide future consulting services to the former employer on such terms as may be agreed upon. None of these terms would be available through a court ruling.[8] Arguably, the parties to a mediation cannot reach a resolution that would be against public policy.

Mediation also allows for tremendous savings in both time and money to both parties, particularly when the mediation is conducted at a relatively early stage of the proceeding. Mediation also allows the parties to avoid or at least minimize the stress that is inherent in litigation.

Even where no settlement is reached, mediation can be a useful tool to both parties as they can learn about the relative strengths and weaknesses of both their own case as well as that of their adversary. The parties may gain a better understanding of the other party's perspective of the dispute. It can serve to reduce the number of issues in dispute. In essence, mediation can amount to a quasi-discovery process. In addition, as part of the mediation process, opponents may receive documents upon which the other party is relying, which they might not otherwise receive at that early stage of the proceeding. Although the Ontario *Rules of Civil Procedure* requires the exchange of affidavit of documents soon after the close of pleadings, the practical reality is that they are often not exchanged until much later. Of course, where mediation takes place and no action has been commenced, there is no requirement of full disclosure of documentation, but it is still smart practice to provide full disclosure.

In addition, through the use of mediation, there are specific benefits that may be uniquely experienced by an employee to a dispute. Whether the legal issues to be resolved relate to the loss of employment or to other employment issues, they are often felt on a deeply emotional level by the employee. The mediation process, by its very nature, can be an extremely therapeutic experience for an aggrieved employee. Due to the informal

---

[8] See Chapter 7, "Creative Resolutions to Employment Law Disputes" for a detailed analysis.

nature of a mediation, the employee may be allowed the opportunity to vent his or her feelings, frustrations and concerns. The ability to be heard may be as important to some employees as are the details of any financial settlement. Through the mediation process, the employee may gain a strong sense of empowerment and restitution.

Where a quick resolution is reached, the employee may benefit greatly from being able to successfully close the chapter of his or her life with the former employer, especially if the dignity of the employee remains intact or has been regained through the process.

There are also substantial benefits to both employees and employers where "workplace mediation" is conducted in an attempt to resolve conflict during the course of an employment relationship. Sometimes this can relate to a conflict between co-workers or a conflict between an employee and management. Workplace mediation can help the parties to communicate more effectively. The process can assist the parties to address the matter in a non-adversarial manner and secure an early resolution prior to an escalation of the issues. It can also help to find the root of the problem that is causing the conflict. The inherently flexible process of mediation works well in resolving these sorts of disputes. It can have the advantage of preserving the employment relationship, which may otherwise have appeared doomed. Other obvious benefits of resolving internal workplace conflict quickly is that it can serve to decrease and prevent absenteeism, reduce short- and long-term disability claims, decrease turnover and support a workplace culture of fairness and equity.

The employee may ultimately benefit from the control he or she exerts over the course of events during the mediation process. In addition, the employee may feel personally and emotionally rewarded as a result of the company's proactive and responsible approach to resolving the dispute. A mediated resolution also leads to countless benefits that are unique to an employer. The employer may be positioned to negotiate protections for itself that would not be available from a court award. For instance, the employer may be able to secure "valuable" restrictive covenants from a terminated employee. In addition, through means of a strict confidentiality clause with respect to the terms of settlement, the employer may be able to resolve the dispute without setting potentially costly precedents. The mediation may allow the employer to resolve the dispute away from the public eye, as litigation can sometimes damage a company's reputation and cause embarrassment to the company and its executives. Where it is known that a company is inclined to mediate disputes fairly, the company may be further rewarded with a boost in employee morale and overall company productivity. Employees will likely perceive an employer's proactive response to the legal dispute in a positive light. The mediation process may also be somewhat educational for an employer who may learn from the process and avoid similar employment-related problems in the future.

7. VOLUNTARY VERSUS MANDATORY MEDIATION

A defining feature of mediation is that both parties to a dispute "voluntarily" participate in the process in an attempt to reach a mutually acceptable result. Despite this, throughout Canada there has been a rise in legislation that provides for court-connected and other "mandatory" mediation programs that must be pursued by the parties before the court will intervene to determine the rights and obligations of the parties. In Ontario, mandatory mediation has been in place in Toronto and Ottawa since 1999 and in Windsor since 2002. This means that all employment law actions in those centres must proceed to mediation within 180 days of the first defence being filed. The litigants can choose from a roster list of mediators or they may jointly select another mediator. The cost of the mediation is borne by the parties.

The introduction of mandatory mediation in Canada has been met with mixed feelings. Supporters of mandatory mediation cite the following advantages:

- the current adversarial court system does not adequately serve the needs of all parties;
- mediation does not preclude other legal avenues or alternative dispute resolution mechanisms;
- the timing of mediation is controlled in mandatory mediation which saves on time and costs;
- disputes resolved in mediation result in a reduction in the already backlogged court docket;
- mediation may result in faster, cheaper and more tailored settlements;
- mediation can be terminated at any time by either party; and
- there is a relatively high success rate in mandatory mediation programs with high ratings of satisfaction.[9]

---

[9] Canadian Bar Association Task Force Report, *Alternative Dispute Resolution: A Canadian Perspective* (Ottawa: Canadian Bar Foundation, 1989), at p. 62; *Alternative Dispute Resolution Manual* (CCH Canadian Ltd., 1998), at paras. 22,760 and 22,805; L. Boulle and K. Kelly, *Mediation: Principles, Process, Practice* (Toronto: Butterworths, 1998), at p. 20.

However, the implementation of mandatory mediation has been subjected to some criticism. Common concerns expressed by opponents of mandatory mediation are:

- mandatory mediation undermines the co-operative and consensual principles inherent in mediation;
- mandatory mediation increases settlement pressures and impairs the ability of the parties to freely accept or reject a particular resolution;
- mandatory mediation may not be an appropriate dispute resolution mechanism for some kinds of disputes;
- mandatory mediation may force unwilling parties to attempt to negotiate which may delay the litigation process and add further costs;
- attaching mediation to the court system results in confusion by the users who expect binding decisions by the court system and not court-sponsored negotiations;
- mediation is not a regulated practice with defined educational requirements;
- mediation may increase the costs by adding a further stage to those matters which were likely to settle on their own; and
- there is a shortage of qualified mediators.[10] (It is important to note that in Ontario and likely in all jurisdictions of Canada, where employment mediations are now being used widely, there are now a large number of qualified mediators, so this concern has been significantly lessened.)

Although now somewhat dated, a survey of users of the Toronto General Division ADR pilot project in 1995 found that one in three clients whose cases settled through the ADR pilot project felt that they had been pressured into a final agreement. However, the data did not establish the source of the pressure, whether from the mediator, counsel or both.[11] It is our view that with greater experience amongst mediators and counsel and greater awareness amongst clients, this apparent pressure should be less prevalent now than it was at the time of the survey.

---

[10] Canadian Bar Association Task Force Report, *ibid.*, at p. 62; Boulle and Kelly, *ibid.*, at p. 19.

[11] J. MacFarlane, *Court-Ordered Mediation in Civil Cases: An Evaluation of the Ontario Court (General Division)* (Toronto: Ontario Ministry of the Attorney General, 1995), at pp. 143-44 and 147.

MEDIATION IN THE EMPLOYMENT LAW SETTING

Unless mediation is court mandated, it will only be utilized in circumstances where the consent of all parties to proceed to mediation has been obtained. In cases where mediation is voluntarily attempted, the outcome may be more successful as it is assumed that all parties are interested in using mediation to bring closure to the issues existing between them.

Chapter 2
DETERMINING WHEN TO MEDIATE

1. GENERAL CONSIDERATIONS

When faced with a legal dispute, it is important at the outset, for counsel and client to assess the client's legal position and goals and to determine the appropriate strategy to effectively achieve those goals. For many kinds of employment law disputes, a useful strategy for implementing one's objectives is to engage in a process of voluntary mediation. However, determining how and when to mediate a dispute is often a very difficult decision. Where the employee hopes to secure the consent of the company to mediate a dispute quickly, is it prudent for the employee's counsel to set out threatening demands or would it be preferable to approach the other side in a more conciliatory manner? Should a legal action be pursued aggressively in the hope of intimidating the opponent into eventually succumbing to mediation and settling the dispute? Should mediation be considered at the outset of a legal dispute, after the close of pleadings, prior to trial or not at all? Once you and your client determine that mediation would be worthwhile, how do you convince the opponent of the merits of mediation? There are no simple answers or clear-cut rules to these questions. The answers will, of course, depend on a number of factors including the nature of the dispute, complexity of the facts and issues and the characteristics of the parties involved in the dispute. Obviously, where mediation is part of the legal process, some of these considerations are irrelevant. However, even where mediation is mandatory, there are many times when the matter is not settled at the mediation stage and the parties are faced with these same questions at a later stage of the proceeding when considering a further round of mediation.

Although not all cases will be suitable for mediation, it is prudent for counsel to at least consider the possibility of mediation in each case. Where early mediation is deemed inappropriate, it is a good practice to evaluate the feasibility of mediation at each successive stage in the proceeding. Of course, even where a determination is made at a certain stage that mediation would be in your client's best interest, it may not be possible to convince your opponent in the particular dispute of the merits of mediation.

Sometimes more than one mediation will take place in a legal matter at different stages of the proceeding. Often, the appetite for settlement increases as the matter proceeds toward trial. Although costly, it can be effective to convene a second mediation either with the same mediator or a new one.

Some mediation experts have argued that there is an ethical obligation on the part of counsel to consider the use of mediation in each legal dispute. It is argued that if there is a probability of satisfactorily resolving a case through mediation, counsel has an ethical duty to apprise his or her client of the process. Whether there exists such a mandatory duty has become a hotly debated issue in the United States. In Ontario, the *Rules of Professional Conduct*[1] for lawyers delineates some degree of ethical obligation on the part of counsel to consider alternative dispute resolutions ("ADR"). Rule 2.02(2) states: "A lawyer shall advise and encourage the client to compromise or settle a dispute whenever it is possible to do so on a reasonable basis and shall discourage the client from commencing useless legal proceedings". Rule 2.02(3) states: "The lawyer shall consider the use of alternative dispute resolution (ADR) for every dispute, and if appropriate, the lawyer shall inform the client of ADR options and, if so instructed, take steps to pursue those options". The movement towards mandatory mediation programs in Canada has worked towards solidifying this obligation, perhaps not so much from an ethical standpoint as much as from a procedural standpoint.

In most employment law cases, the parties will exchange their respective positions through carefully scripted correspondence and at least some degree of negotiation will take place between the parties before mediation is attempted. However, there may be some occasions in employment law where mediation may be appropriate even before any negotiations have taken place and before the parties have been clearly apprised of their opponent's positions. We will discuss some of these circumstances in this chapter and will provide some helpful guidelines as to when and in what context counsel should consider the mediation option in the conduct of an employment law dispute. Assessing the suitability and timing of mediation to a dispute are of paramount concern.

---

[1] Law Society of Upper Canada, *Rules of Professional Conduct*, effective November 1, 2000.

22

DETERMINING WHEN TO MEDIATE

(a) Suitability

In assessing the suitability of mediation to a particular employment law matter, obvious considerations include the type of dispute and the particular personality traits, needs, interests and objectives of the parties. Mediation may be favoured by a party who is concerned about any one or more of the following: negative publicity, the preservation of a continuing relationship, the cost of litigation, the increasing *quantum* of damages or the disappearance of evidence and/or witnesses. On the other hand, mediation may not be appropriate where one or more of the following circumstances exists: where there are overriding public policy considerations that might benefit from a judgment or a decision of a court or tribunal, elements of criminality, elements of personal danger or severe power imbalances between the parties.

The following chart may be helpful in assessing whether mediation is an appropriate avenue for a particular case:

Suitability	Unsuitability
Moderate degree of conflict	Severe degree of conflict
Continuing relationship or potentially salvageable one	Very acrimonious relationship*
Power balance/moderate imbalance	Severe power imbalance
Multiple issues of fact and law	Single or few legal issues*
Party ability/emotional stability	Severe emotional instability
Proper motivation of the parties	Ulterior motives
Factual/legal issues in dispute	Significant public policy issues
Safety of parties	Personal danger/criminal element
Cost/time conscious	Not concerned about cost/time
Avoidance of publicity	Publicity seeking

* It should be noted that having either an acrimonious relationship or addressing only a single legal issue, on its own does not make a matter unsuitable for mediation. Mediation may still be suitable but these are just two factors that need to be considered as part of the whole.

(b) The Importance of Timing

In principle, mediation may take place at any stage of a legal proceeding. It should be noted that it is arguably never too late to consider mediation, even on the eve of trial. The more pertinent question often is — how early in the proceeding is it too soon to consider mediation? The answer will depend on the unique circumstances of each case. Where the parties intend to continue their employment relationship, mediation may be most appropriate at a very early stage of the proceeding, possibly even before any negotiations have taken place and without the need for any extensive communication of the parties' respective interests and needs. Even where the parties are not continuing the employment relationship, there may still be circumstances where mediation will be appropriate at a very early stage in the proceeding. For instance, the parties may be interested in preserving positive business relations, despite the fact that the employment relationship has terminated, and they may be fearful that litigation will destroy their mutual goodwill and respect. Where parties are concerned about the potential publicity of a lawsuit, an early mediation may also be desired.

Despite the merits of mediating a dispute early and avoiding the inherent cost and time delays of litigation, some cases will not easily lend themselves to early mediation. In these cases, at an early stage, the parties may not yet feel the true risk of litigation and consequently, will make no real attempt to settle the matter. The issues and the evidence may not yet be clearly defined. In these circumstances, early mediation may be a waste of time and money. In some cases, it may be necessary to commence litigation before mediation will be effective. Some parties will only truly appreciate the seriousness of the issues and the intentions of their opponent after this aggressive and definitive step has been taken. Sometimes the key to achieving a reasonable settlement for your client is to make it clear to the opponent that you are ready, willing and able to try the case.

However, it is wise to never completely close the door to mediation. Mediation may take place at a very late stage in the proceeding including after the trial has been completed and before the court's decision has been rendered.

It is significant to note that one U.S. study determined that the stage of the litigation where mediation takes place does not seem to make a significant difference in the settlement rates.[2]

The following chart may be helpful in assessing the appropriate time to mediate a particular dispute:

---

[2]   "Statistics on Mediation in the 101st District Court as of June 12, 1992", as condensed in *Court Annexed Mediation* (State Bar of Texas Minimum Continuing Legal Education, 1993).

Stage	Suitability/Appropriateness
pre-negotiation stage	— where there is a continuing relationship between the parties; cost and timing are serious considerations; informal mediation process is preferred; non-complicated facts and issues or easily defined issues. Also where one or both sides would like to avoid publicity, such as in the case of allegations of harassment that could reflect badly on either one or both of the employee and the employer
post-negotiation/pre-pleading stage	— where there is a continuing relationship between the parties; multiple issues that are not overly complex; appearance of some concessions on both sides; issues and needs are somewhat defined; cost and timing are factors
post-pleading/pre-discovery stage	— issues and needs have been defined and/or narrowed through pleadings; not overly complex such that discovery not essential to narrow the issues
post-discovery/pre-trial stage	— issues are complex but have been narrowed by discovery; weighing of risks in favour of mediation; where trial would be lengthy and complex; avoidance of the costs and risks of trial; avoidance of negative publicity which may be occasioned by trial
post-trial/pre-judgment stage	— weighing of risks in favour of mediated solution; avoidance of unfavourable ruling and cost consequences against unsuccessful party; where no indication of clear winner at trial; where unsuccessful party is likely to appeal

2. DETERMINING THE ISSUES

As delineated in the first chapter, there are a multitude of legal and factual issues that can be encountered in the employment law setting. In this chapter, we will outline a number of scenarios a lawyer may be faced with in the course of practising employment law. We will in turn discuss the appropriateness of the mediation option to resolving each type of dispute. We will also suggest the most preferred context of the mediation as well as the most beneficial timing of the mediation in each scenario.

25

In the practice of employment law, you as counsel will most often be consulted by a client, whether an employee or an employer, following the termination of the employment relationship. At this time, with your client's input, you will engage in a process of assessing your client's rights and obligations and determining the appropriate course of action. However, at other times, you will be retained by an employee or employer who is seeking advice on the handling of a dispute that arises during the course of an employment relationship.

We will divide this section into two distinct groups — those situations where an employment relationship is continuing between the parties, and those where the relationship between the parties has been terminated. The format, context and timing of the mediation will typically vary depending on the category within which the matter falls.

(a)   Continuing Employment Relationship — The Concept of "Workplace Mediation"

When mediation was first used to mediate employment disputes, it was normally in the context of resolving legal issues that arose from a terminated employment relationship. However, over the last several years, mediation has been increasingly used in the context of resolving issues (both legal and non-legal) between an employee and an employer during an existing employment relationship. As we have outlined, there is a wide spectrum of issues that can arise at the workplace during the course of an employment relationship. No matter how fair, equitable and proactive their practices may be no employer is immune from these problems. It is important for employers to step "out of the box" of traditional employee management and consider workplace mediation as a means of resolving internal workplace disputes and preserving a deteriorating employment relationship (and many now are doing so). It is possible that many performance issues an employer perceives as being beyond rectification may in fact be resolved through the use of informal workplace mediation. In many circumstances, it may cost an employer far less to repair a strained employment relationship than to recruit and train a replacement employee.

Many employers have developed internal workplace complaint procedures to assist employees to deal with issues that arise in the course of their employment. These internal procedures allow employees to voice their concerns and to have them addressed through a number of different means. One of the preferred methods of addressing and resolving such concerns is through a process of informal workplace mediation.

DETERMINING WHEN TO MEDIATE

Despite its obvious benefits, many employers in Canada do not have a workplace dispute resolution process in place. However, by taking these proactive steps to deal with inevitable workplace issues, employers may derive substantial cost savings in the long run. The process may also serve to boost employee morale, increase productivity and diffuse difficult employment situations.

There are a substantial number of training programs available for human resources professionals and other interested individuals to receive specialized instruction on conducting workplace mediations. Where warranted, having a trained workplace mediator on board can ultimately save an employer a lot of friction, turmoil, energy and money as well as the obvious benefits derived from a workforce that feels that their workplace is fair and equitable. Larger employers may find this training to be a very worthwhile endeavour.

For smaller employers, or in more complex cases, there are a number of experienced human resources consultants who are available to be hired to conduct neutral third party mediations. Even where an in-house trained person exists, there are some circumstances where a problem can be more effectively resolved through a workplace mediation conducted by a neutral third party mediator than by an in-house person. Some cases may simply not be appropriate for an in-house representative.

(i) *Workplace dispute policy*

The philosophy behind a workplace dispute policy is that the traditional legal adversarial system is rarely the best means of dispute resolution in the workplace. By its nature, litigation tends to drive parties apart and in doing so, weakens their relationship. Often, the litigation process completely ignores the underlying problem and if the parties have a chance at a continuing relationship, addressing the underlying problem is critical. Since minor disagreements and the stresses inherent in employment relationships can escalate to the point of termination of employment, a proactive approach to managing these problems at an early stage can avoid this often undesirable result.

Over the last two or three decades, employment litigation has vastly increased in Canada. This is partly due to the increasing rights and obligations of the parties to an employment relationship, the competitive business environment and the ever-changing public policy surrounding employment law issues. There is an evolving body of legislation that impact employer and employee relations. As a result, added pressure has been placed on employers as they strive to successfully manage their staff in an increasingly competitive, demanding and changing environment.

By adopting a workplace dispute policy, employers are often able to deal with potential lawsuits before they ever get to that stage. In fact, many issues can be satisfactorily dealt with at an early stage before there is a need for either party to involve legal counsel. Matters can also be dealt with in an effort to salvage the employment relationship before it sours beyond repair. The written policy often encompasses a series of progressive steps or options, which may include an open door policy, formal internal grievance procedures, mediation, fact finding, peer review and finally, arbitration. Each employer should adapt the policy to best suit its own interests and the interests of its employees, taking into account the size and nature of the company, the atmosphere and characteristics of the workforce.

An "open door policy" can be very simple to implement. It may simply be a statement of policy that the employer encourages all employees to discuss any concern with his or her supervisor or higher level of management, without the fear of reprisal. The nature of the employee concern can be very wide-ranging and may be as simple as a perceived personality conflict with a co-worker or supervisor. Often, minor disputes can be successfully resolved at this preliminary stage. However, in the absence of an internal dispute resolution mechanism, the issue might have otherwise festered and become increasingly problematic, leading to the eventual termination of the employment relationship. One thing to keep in mind is that an open door policy is meaningless unless the employer actually promotes it and puts it in use.

The typical second step involves the filing of a formal complaint where an employee can challenge aspects of his or her employment. This can be in relation to a term of employment, issue of harassment or discrimination or a perceived conflict with a co-worker. The policy should clearly specify the complaint procedure and the appeals procedure to progressively higher levels of management who are called upon to adjudicate the employee's concerns. This process may be utilized as a first step in the process or following the open door approach where an employee is not satisfied with the outcome of that approach. Where appropriate, the complaint may require an external investigation to determine the "facts".

The third step of a typical workplace dispute policy is workplace mediation. This would normally be available to an employee where he or she is not satisfied with the outcome of the internal complaint procedure. The policy should specify the manner of the mediation, how it is arranged, how the costs are borne and what materials are required. The policy may allow for a very informal mediation for certain kinds of disputes or a formal mediation involving an experienced, neutral third party mediator where the circumstances of the matter, sensitivity or seriousness of the allegations require it. It should be kept in mind that if a complaint has been filed, an investigation should take place before mediation is attempted. If the findings of the complaint are substantiated and the matter is serious, termination of one or more parties may be inevitable, in which case a workplace mediation may not be appropriate. Where a workplace mediation is deemed appropriate, it will often be effective at helping the parties to find ways to interact and work together in the future.

An alternative step may involve a process of peer review. With this step, the parties submit a dispute or issue to a panel of peers or a combination of peers and managers for formal assessment and evaluation, which may be binding. This is an idea that is likely used very rarely. Although the concept has some merit, it does present potential problems with confidentiality and neutrality. Practically speaking, a lot of employees may refrain from filing a complaint if they knew it would be subject to a peer review. On the flip side, some employees may actively campaign for the support of their peers. This could certainly be disruptive to the workplace. Employers and employees should therefore be cautioned before submitting to this process.

In the final stage, a more formal process of arbitration may be used where earlier attempts at resolution have not been effective. In arbitration, the parties present their dispute to a third party who hears the evidence and arguments of the parties and renders a binding decision. The policy should specify how the arbitration is arranged, how it is conducted and how costs are shared. Arbitration can be a very effective method of dispute resolution in the workplace. Not only is it commonly used in labour disputes, but it is commonly used in disputes arising from the interpretation of employment contracts.

Of course, where an employer implements an internal workplace dispute policy, it must be widely distributed and publicized to all staff members. In order to be effective, such a policy must receive the support of senior management and the appropriate structure and mechanisms must be in place to ensure the fair, objective and consistent use of the dispute resolution system.[3] This, of course, includes an education and training aspect for managers and staff members.

---

[3] See Appendix 2A for a checklist for developing an internal workplace dispute policy.

Although we have set out the dispute policy as a series of progressive steps, it may be preferable to set out a few alternative options for resolution and give the employee and employer the opportunity to choose the preferred option.

(ii) *Performance issues/Disciplinary measures*

It is not uncommon for a lawyer to be consulted by an employee who is disgruntled upon receiving a negative performance review or upon the imposition of a disciplinary penalty. The disciplinary measure may involve a warning, probationary period or suspension. From the employee's perspective, upon the receipt of a negative performance review, it is important that he or she takes a proactive stance by providing a written rebuttal to any untrue, unfair or out-of-context statements in his or her performance review. Upon the imposition of a disciplinary penalty, it is important that the employee provides a reasonable explanation for any alleged wrongdoing for which a penalty has been imposed. The imposition of a probationary period or suspension usually carries with it the clear threat of termination. It is therefore essential that any such rebuttal be provided by the disgruntled employee in a timely manner. Since there is an existing employment relationship, it is usually preferable for you as counsel to not become directly involved in the dispute at this stage. However, you can provide helpful "behind the scenes" assistance. You may assist your client by providing guidance with respect to the contents of the rebuttal and ensuring that the proper protections are in place and the appropriate relief is sought. Often, a lawyer will be retained to "ghost write" such a rebuttal. In terms of relief, the employee may seek to have the performance documentation revised or the penalty removed from his or her employment record.

From the employer's perspective, a substandard performance review is often the first step in building a case for just cause against an employee, based on poor or unsatisfactory performance. Most employers have learned the importance of a well-documented performance management program to support a decision of termination on the basis of poor performance. Where the performance management has advanced to the stage of probation or suspension, the employer may perceive termination of the employment relationship as a foregone conclusion. Employers may not have considered the concept of mediation as a means of resolving such performance disputes as an alternative to immediate termination. In reality, the perceived performance issues may be the result of a misunderstanding, poor communication or a personality conflict between the employee and supervisor, rather than due to true performance deficiencies. Employers should realize that the matter may be easily remedied through workplace mediation. Poor performance can also be indicative of difficulties in the employee's personal life, including health, family, financial and marital issues. A mediation would give an opportunity for the parties to discuss relevant matters and develop ways that the employer might be able to help the employee and develop reasonable expectations for performance over a reasonable period of time. It goes without saying that employees who feel that they are under scrutiny often face increasingly troubled performance.

Where the employee has provided a rebuttal to the employer's actions but is not satisfied with the ongoing relationship, it may be prudent for you, as employee's counsel, to assess the matter with a view to promoting a workplace mediation. You must assess the interests, needs and objectives of your client. Where a determination is made that workplace mediation is appropriate, you should consider the context and format of the mediation. Where the issues appear simple, informal workplace mediation with a human resources employee may be satisfactory. However, it should be noted that many employees will deem a human resources professional to be lacking in the requisite degree of neutrality as they are really acting as a "voice" of management.

Where informal workplace mediation is preferred, counsel may not become involved in the mediation process on a direct basis. However, you may be involved to the extent of providing the requisite degree of guidance and coaching to your client in advance of the informal workplace mediation session. It should be noted that this form of mediation may not be appropriate in a small company where no human resources department exists or where the human resources department does not have the sophistication, objectivity or experience to oversee the mediation process. It may also not be appropriate where termination of employment appears imminent or the issues faced are serious. In these circumstances, a formal workplace mediation may be preferred, utilizing the services of a neutral third party mediator and possibly the direct involvement of counsel.

Mediations in these circumstances may allow the parties to resolve a dispute amicably with the overriding objective of preserving the employment relationship. In many cases of this nature, mediation allows the parties to attempt to understand each other's positions and discuss the appropriateness of any penalty. The informality and unstructured nature of the workplace mediation will allow for maximum flexibility in the conduct of the mediation. A mediation of this kind would most easily fall within the transformative model discussed in Chapter 1. Often, even in circumstances where the employer and the employee are of the view that termination is inevitable, clear communication and the expression of expectations and interests may still salvage a deteriorating relationship.

(iii) *Human rights issues*

Employment law counsel is frequently retained to deal with human rights disputes that unfortunately continue to arise in the workplace despite increasing awareness of rights and responsibilities. Sometimes these disputes are the result of misunderstandings or poor communications between employees rather than a result of direct discrimination. These situations are well suited to resolution through mediation. Even where there is evidence that discrimination has occurred, mediation is often an appropriate means to resolution of the dispute. However, where an employee feels that his or her human rights have been infringed, the employee may choose to file a complaint with the applicable human rights body. As will be discussed in detail in Chapter 8, the Ontario Human Rights Tribunal encourages the resolution of these complaints through mediation.

Sexual harassment

Sexual harassment is one of the most insidious forms of discrimination. It has been shown that unwelcome sexual conduct can lead to serious repercussions on the emotional well-being of the victim and can lead to significant impact upon his or her morale and work productivity. It is not surprising that sexual harassment in the workplace is a concern of both employees and employers. It is prohibited conduct under human rights legislation in every jurisdiction of Canada. Today, most employers have broad harassment and discrimination policies which define not only the nature of the prohibited conduct but also the procedures to be followed when an alleged infraction occurs. In some harassment policies, mediation is clearly delineated as one of the available means to resolving a harassment dispute. However, even where it is not stipulated, mediation may be a suitable means of resolving a harassment dispute, both vis-à-vis the complainant and respondent and vis-à-vis the complainant and the employer.

Where an incident of sexual harassment occurs in the workplace, you as counsel may be consulted by the victim of sexual harassment, the alleged accused or the employer that is facing a sexual harassment complaint. The nature and extent of your involvement will vary depending on the seriousness and complexity of the matter. It will also depend on which party to the matter you have been hired to represent. In most cases, where a complaint arises, a thorough and timely investigation will take place by the employer, its counsel or a neutral third party investigator. Where the results of the investigation warrant it, a penalty may be imposed on the alleged accused. Often, it is determined through the investigation that changes in work processes or reporting relationships are required which may impact upon the alleged accused and the complainant. It is often difficult for the employer to determine the appropriate solution, and in certain cases mediation may be a means of satisfying all parties to the dispute. A careful analysis should be conducted by you to determine whether mediation is an appropriate option for your client. In cases of sexual harassment, this determination may be more difficult than most. It would normally be premature to consider mediation prior to the completion of the investigation. Whether mediation is appropriate will depend on the particular circumstances of the case and the findings of the investigator. Although the mediation of a sexual harassment matter may often be effective, it should be kept in mind that parties' emotions usually run very high and the potential damages may not be readily quantifiable at an early stage, especially where the victim has suffered severe mental distress. You must carefully consider whether mediation is in your client's best interest. Not all sexual harassment matters will be suited to mediation. In some cases, the victim may not want to confront the alleged accused in a face-to-face, voluntary mediation in an attempt to resolve the matter and may instead prefer other available remedies such as formally filing a human rights complaint or seeking a departure from the employer. If not handled properly, the emotional well-being of the individuals involved can be negatively impacted.

If it is determined that mediation is indeed the appropriate course of action, the utilization of an experienced third party mediator with specialized experience in dealing with matters of this nature will be preferable to an internal mediator. You, as counsel may be actively involved, particularly where your client requires substantial "hand-holding" and guidance because of the nature of the issues or your client's emotional vulnerability. Time will generally be of the essence in diffusing the situation, particularly where the parties are interested in preserving the employment relationship. However, where one of the parties is very emotional or distressed, it may be necessary to delay the mediation until the party is better able to cope with the inherent demands of mediation.

In many cases of this nature, there will be at least three parties — the victim, the accused and the employer. The number of parties involved may impact on the manner of and conduct of the mediation to a certain extent.

Disability

Disability issues that arise in the employment setting can be very wide-ranging. Disability is a protected ground under the human rights legislation of every jurisdiction in Canada and forms the basis of more human rights complaints than most other grounds. Any employee who feels that his or her rights have been infringed in the workplace on the basis of disability has the undisputed right to file a complaint with the applicable human rights commission. However, issues of disability are often dealt with between employees and employers without filing a formal complaint. It is not surprising that in their practices, employment counsel often confront issues of this nature. You may be approached by a disabled employee who expresses concerns about discriminatory conduct or a lack of accommodation by the employer at the workplace. You may at other times be consulted by an employer with a view to obtaining guidance on the handling of difficult issues involving a disabled employee or one who has unexpectedly commenced a sick leave. Where there is a dispute over an issue of disability, regardless of who you represent, after the facts have been gathered and the appropriate investigation has been completed, you should immediately assess whether the dispute can be addressed through workplace mediation. Of foremost importance in the determination of whether workplace mediation is appropriate is whether the parties intend to preserve the employment relationship. Also important is a consideration of the nature of the issues in question. Where the issue relates to the accommodation of the disabled employee, this may require physical changes to the work environment, the granting of additional rest periods, the modification of the hours of work or granting the employee the flexibility to work from home. Accommodation issues are often readily resolvable through workplace mediation. A simple process of brainstorming to find workable solutions may suffice. However, if the allegations of discrimination are serious, the relationship has been severely strained or there is inflexibility in the parties' positions, the relationship between the parties may not be salvageable. Even so, the mediation process may be worthwhile as the parties may reach a satisfactory resolution through mediation, which would allow them to terminate the employment relationship on mutually agreeable terms.

Sometimes, a mediation allows for a smooth and desired exit from the employment relationship.

If mediation is a viable option, the format of the mediation will depend on the seriousness of the allegations and the characteristics of the parties. If the dispute is considered a minor disagreement between the parties, informal workplace mediation may be preferable and if so, the mediation may proceed on an in-house basis with the use of trained human resources professionals. However, where the issues are more contentious, the allegations serious or the relationship strained, it may be advisable to pursue a more formal mediation process with the use of a third party mediator who has the requisite experience to deal with sensitive and specialized issues of disability and accommodation. The appropriate timing of the mediation will also need to be assessed. In most cases, the earliest possible mediation date would be preferred, especially in circumstances where diffusing the difficult situation is important to both parties. It will be in both parties' interest to ensure that a disabled employee is being treated fairly and that all necessary protections for that employee are in place.

Pregnancy/Parental leave

Every jurisdiction of Canada imposes strict rules regarding an employer's obligations to employees who are either pregnant, on pregnancy or parental leave or intending to take pregnancy or parental leave. Essentially, employers are prohibited from directly or indirectly discriminating against employees or punishing, penalizing or treating employees differently as a result of taking a pregnancy or parental leave. These obligations and rights are imposed in each jurisdiction both through employment standards legislation and human rights legislation. Upon an employee's return to work from pregnancy or parental leave, employment standards legislation requires an employer to return the employee to the same position that he or she held prior to the leave or to a comparable position if the employee's previous position no longer exists within the organization. Because of the scope of the legal rights and obligations, it is not surprising that issues relating to pregnancy and parental leave frequently arise between an employer and an employee.

The kinds of issues that may arise during an employee's pregnancy or parental leave include allegations of unfair treatment. For instance, this may apply where an employee has failed to receive a salary increase, has been demoted or has been passed over for a promotion. Issues may also arise where the employer has failed to make reasonable accommodations for an employee for health-related concerns during the course of her pregnancy. Also, a common dispute surrounds apparent changes to an employee's position or a failure to return an employee to his or her position following a return from pregnancy or parental leave.

It is not difficult to imagine the useful application of workplace mediation to resolving problems of this nature. From the employer's perspective, mediation may be an important means of diffusing a potential conflict, improving morale and preserving a positive employment relationship. The employee may have similar interests in mind. However, because strict obligations are imposed on the employer through legislation, which allows for substantial remedies in favour of an employee, the employee may have added incentive to proceed with a formal statutory complaint rather than submit to mediation. Accordingly, when acting for an employee, in addition to the usual considerations in assessing the appropriateness of mediation, you should seriously consider with your client the pros and cons of mediation versus filing a formal statutory complaint. Of course, mediation may still be an option at some point after filing statutory complaints. It is possible that a mediated solution at an early stage of the dispute will be more conducive to preserving and improving an employment relationship if that is the objective of the parties. It should be noted that the filing of a complaint in and of itself should not preclude the possibility of mediation at a later date. The timing, format and strategy of the mediation will, of course, depend on the seriousness of the issues, urgency of the matter and objectives of the parties. Because of the specialized nature of the issues and the potential damages, a third party mediation will generally be preferable to an informal internal mediation and if so, counsel for both parties will likely play an active role in the mediation process.

Other forms of discrimination and harassment

There are a number of other forms of discrimination an employee may face during the course of an employment relationship for which legal counsel may be consulted. These may include allegations of discrimination by a fellow employee, supervisor or the company. It may also include allegations that a work atmosphere has become poisoned. Workplace harassment is generally defined as behaviour that demeans, embarrasses, humiliates, annoys or abuses a person and that is known or reasonably expected to be unwelcome. This applies even if such behaviour is not related to a protected ground. This can also include behaviour that constitutes bullying, which is an area that has received increasing awareness in recent years. It can also include workplace violence, which is protected by legislation in some provinces.

As previously mentioned, many employers have formal written anti-harassment and anti-discrimination policies that may set forth a comprehensive complaint procedure. Mediation may be set out as an option in the written policy. Whether you are consulted by the victim, alleged accused or the employer, a determination should be made as to the appropriateness of mediation to resolving the dispute. Where mediation is deemed appropriate, in most cases, it would be advisable to use a third party mediator with the appropriate set of skills to deal with cases of this nature. In most cases, the mediation should take place at the earliest possible date, especially if the parties wish to preserve the employment relationship. In discrimination cases it is also important that any improper behaviour or conduct cease, and for this reason early intervention is critical.

However, where the allegations are very serious or the atmosphere has become severely poisoned to the extent that there appear to be no viable solutions, mediation may not be appropriate at an early stage. In some cases, it may be in the best interest of the complainant to file a formal complaint with the Human Rights Tribunal. As discussed earlier, in Ontario, the Human Rights Tribunal encourages the parties to attempt to mediate solutions to disputes. These mediations are handled by vice-chairs of the tribunal who have the skills required to facilitate an appropriate solution. It should be noted that in some cases of alleged discrimination, broad public policy issues may arise which may not be easily dealt with through mediation. This will be discussed in greater detail in Chapter 8, "Special Issues in Mediating Employment Law Disputes".

(iv) Constructive dismissal

A particularly grey area of employment law involves the concept of constructive dismissal. An employee may assert that he or she has been constructively dismissed where the employer has caused substantial changes to the terms and conditions of employment, such as a salary decrease, demotion, significant reduction in role and responsibilities, or a change in reporting structure, among other things. Where an employer has imposed changes to an employee's job, the employee may face a very difficult decision. Often, with the assistance of counsel, the employee must quickly decide whether to accept the changes to his or her position in mitigation of damages or assert the position that the employment relationship has been fundamentally breached by the employer. Although the courts have considered issues involving constructive dismissal innumerable times, few clear-cut rules have been established.

During the recession in 2009, we advised many employers on changes to employment terms that were necessitated by economic conditions. Some employers sought to avoid terminations and instead chose to reduce hours and salaries across all staff. Many of these employers invoked informal discussions (akin to an informal mediation) to broach the matters with employees.

Where you are acting for an employee in circumstances of potential constructive dismissal, you and your client may wish to consider the possibility of mediation before your client even makes a decision whether to accept or reject such changes. There may be an opportunity to present the issue to the employer and resolve the dispute through mediation, with a view to preserving the employment relationship on mutually agreeable terms. It is possible that the employer's actions in imposing these changes to an employee's job were purely innocent. The employer may not have anticipated that such a change would result in a negative reaction from the employee and the employer may be willing to discuss other opportunities with the employee that may be satisfactory to both parties. In these circumstances, mediation may be a viable means of negotiating fair terms for the position. If so, the mediation may take a very informal tone and may be conducted with the assistance of the company's human resources department. At times, it may be preferable to retain a third party mediator, especially if a lot is at stake for the parties or there appears to be considerable division between the positions. Where the employer determines that the changes are necessary, the mediation may also lead to a mutually agreeable severance package with the assistance of a mediator.

However, other times, the employer may possess a "take it or leave it" attitude and construe any rejection of the changes by the employee, whether direct or indirect, as a resignation of employment. If this occurs, the employment relationship may not be salvageable. Even so, mediation may still be an option at a later date following the termination of the employment relationship in the course of a wrongful/constructive dismissal dispute. In this context, a third party mediation would be recommended with the active involvement of counsel for both parties.

(v) *Contract dispute during the course of employment*

Many employment relationships are governed by written employment contracts. These are being used increasingly by employers. Even where no written employment agreement exists, there will exist implied terms of employment between an employee and employer. Terms of employment may include terms with respect to compensation, job description, and hours of work, vacation and reporting relationship, among many other things. Where an employee disputes a term of employment (whether written or implied), or alleges the breach of a term of employment, the traditional reaction would be to make the assertion that the employee has been wrongfully or constructively dismissed and is thereby proceeding to commence a legal action. This course of action would generally lead to the immediate termination of the employment relationship.

However, another "softer" and less traditional approach may be to consider a process of workplace mediation in circumstances of constructive dismissal, in an effort to salvage the employment relationship. Informal workplace mediation may be appropriate especially where the employer has not acted out of malice in imposing such changes but pursuant to its genuine business interests. The employer may not have anticipated the employee's reaction to such changes and may be more than willing to resolve the matter through the constructive and cooperative discussions inherent in the mediation process. The mediation may be conducted in an informal manner with the help of human resources or with a third party mediator. Where substantial changes exist or a large amount of money is in dispute, it will often be preferable to retain the services of a third party mediator and actively involve counsel for both parties in the mediation process.

The following chart may be helpful in determining whether a mediation should proceed informally with the assistance of the human resources department or by retaining a third party mediator for workplace mediations, meaning those arising during the course of an existing employment relationship. The chart also summarizes the circumstances where the active involvement of counsel may be preferred:

Human Resources Department

- objectivity/neutrality can be maintained
- where HR is experienced, skilled and has received special training in dispute resolution
- issues are simple

- dispute directly involves fellow employee or supervisor rather than company
- both parties wish to preserve relationship
- cost/timing are important

Third Party Mediator Recommended

- difficult or controversial issues
- HR not experienced, no special dispute resolution training or there are concerns about objectivity/neutrality
- uncertainty of salvageability of relationship
- dispute involves more than two parties
- statutory complaint or lawsuit has been filed
- termination of the relationship is very likely

Involvement of Counsel Recommended

- difficult, serious, complex or sophisticated issues
- one or more parties wish the relationship to terminate
- third party mediator is being used
- statutory complaint or lawsuit has been filed or contemplated
- cost is not a primary concern
- emotional stability of client is a concern
- client requires hand-holding and direct guidance
- a lot of money is at stake

(b) Terminated Employment Relationship

Although workplace mediations are becoming increasingly common and have wide application, the more typical and common application of the mediation process is in resolving legal disputes following the termination of the employment relationship. These are the scenarios for which counsel and employers are more familiar with the use of mediation. In these circumstances, mediation will usually proceed in the more traditional, formal manner with the assistance of a skilled third party mediator. Nonetheless, in cases where the employment relationship has ended, you as counsel must still consider whether mediation is appropriate in view of the particular circumstances of a case and if so, at what stage of the proceeding it would be most appropriate. Of course, in jurisdictions with mandatory mediation, counsel may not be able to dictate when the mediation will take place.

DETERMINING WHEN TO MEDIATE

(i)   *Termination without just cause*

In the vast majority of terminations, no just cause exists nor is it alleged by the employer. Even where the employer thinks it has cause, it will often not take a position of cause unless it can clearly be made out from the facts and evidence. Counsel will not usually recommend a cause termination in the absence of a thorough investigation and definitive, objective findings. As discussed in the previous chapter, a number of factual and legal issues may arise in the context of a termination without cause, the most notable of which is a determination of what is the appropriate notice period. When you are retained or consulted by a terminated employee, an assessment of the case and a determination of the potential damages must be made. The typical first step in the legal proceeding involves sending a threatening demand letter to the employer that clearly sets out the client's legal position. Normally, you will not suggest mediation at this early stage of the matter as there may be a reluctance on the part of your client to appear overly conciliatory. However, there may be circumstances when a non-traditional approach should be taken and you may choose to fashion a more conciliatory demand letter that recommends mediation at the outset of the proceeding. The foremost consideration will always be how you can achieve the best result for your client. On the flip side, there may be circumstances (although rare) where the employer may recommend mediation at this very early stage of the matter upon receipt of a demand letter or other communication of the employee's interests. Many employers are concerned about appearing conciliatory at this early stage and they often prefer a process of legal posturing. It is difficult to provide any rules or guidelines as to when pre-negotiation mediation may be helpful. However, where both parties wish to resolve the matter quickly and avoid the costs of litigation, early mediation may be a useful tool.

In most cases, at least some amount of negotiation will be attempted between the parties before mediation is considered and in many disputes, mediation is not canvassed until the pleadings and discoveries have been completed. Should mediation not be engaged in at this early stage of the proceeding, it should be regularly revisited and reconsidered by counsel at each subsequent stage in the proceeding. Whether mediation is attempted and at what stage will depend on a number of factors.[4]

---

[4]   See charts in this chapter on suitability and timing of mediation.

(ii) *Termination with just cause*

As discussed in the previous chapter, terminations where just cause is alleged by the employer are not clear-cut legal matters and are often hindered with uncertainties for both the employee and employer. When representing a terminated employee, usually the first communication that you have with the company is through your threatening demand letter. However, oftentimes, you and your client are greatly disadvantaged by a lack of facts and information surrounding the allegations of cause. In the normal course of a legal action, this information comes to your attention through the pleadings, document disclosure and examination for discovery.

Typically, mediation may be considered at some point as a means to resolving a legal action for wrongful dismissal and will always be attempted in jurisdictions with mandatory mediation. Because of the inherent uncertainty of the outcome of just cause cases and the fact that a trial will result in a clear winner and loser, many parties would prefer to settle at some stage of the proceeding rather than take on the risk of trial. In cases of cause, there may be a real incentive for the employee to participate in an early mediation. They often feel very "wronged" by the cause termination and a mediation allows for a potential early resolution. It may also allow the employee to become better informed of the nature of the allegations and the strength of the case the employer has against the employee. Where mediation is successful, it also allows the employee to resolve the matter quickly, which may be important to the employee for financial, emotional and professional reasons. The employee can get on with his or her life and career much more quickly than he or she can with a cause termination on record.

When you are representing the employer, the pivotal question may be whether an early mediation would be perceived by the other side as a sign of weakness. Employers often want to present a "tough guy" image when it comes to issues of cause and policy reasons may exist for which they do not wish to appear overly lenient.

Where early mediation is not an option for one or both of the parties, it should be reconsidered at each ensuing stage of the proceeding. Experience dictates that the further the action proceeds, the more likely the reluctant party will be to see the merits of attempting mediation.

(iii) *Allegations of discrimination or harassment raised following termination*

For a variety of reasons, employees often wait until termination occurs before raising issues of discrimination or harassment that had existed or had been perceived to exist during the course of employment. Of course, often the employer has known nothing of the allegations of harassment until after the employee has been terminated. Other times, it is alleged that the act of terminating is discriminatory. These issues often add greater complexity to a wrongful dismissal claim. Cases of this nature generally lend themselves well to the mediation process and early intervention may be preferable for both the employee and the employer in order to address the allegations and determine the substantive issues between them. Often, a global resolution can be achieved on all issues between the parties and the employee is provided with the satisfaction that his or her concerns have been adequately voiced and addressed.

(iv) *Disability arising after termination*

It is also not uncommon for issues of disability to arise after an employee has been terminated. Sometimes, an employee does not appreciate the full extent of his or her disability until termination occurs or the employee has remained silent about his or her disability until the termination occurs. Sometimes, the disability hinders performance which ultimately results in termination. However, if the employer had known about the disability, it may not have proceeded with termination. Other times, an employee becomes ill shortly after termination and within the applicable notice period either as a result of the stress of termination or completely unrelated to the termination. Whatever the circumstances, cases involving issues of disability can be very complicated. Mediation at an early stage may be helpful, especially where all parties wish to jointly determine what the best course of action is with respect to the interplay between disability income and severance pay. If so, it may be necessary to include the disability carrier in the mediation process. It will usually be in the interest of the parties, including the disability carrier, to mediate the matter at the earliest possible stage. However, practically speaking, it is often important that full production of medical documentation has been completed and the employee's condition has been properly assessed and this typically takes considerable time. It is possible that full production will not be available until discoveries are underway and this may delay any worthwhile early attempt at mediation. Another issue to consider is whether the employer becomes the "de facto" insurer if an employee becomes disabled during the notice period and where the employer failed to continue benefits.

(v)   *Violation of post-employment obligations*

As discussed in the last chapter, issues surrounding the application of restrictive covenants often arise in employment matters. An employer may take action against a former employee where it becomes aware that the employee has violated his or her restrictive covenants. Mediation may be a useful means of quickly resolving disputes of this nature. In view of the substantial cost of injunctions both in terms of monetary and non-monetary terms, and in particular the amount of time and money that must be dedicated to such a proceeding at the early stages, early mediation may be a worthwhile consideration for both parties. In addition, the employer will be most interested in a quick resolution as time delays will allow for further potential damage to its business interests. For instance, if a former employee is soliciting the employer's customers, the employer will want a resolution (if not an order or judgment) as quickly as possible to prevent further infractions and the potential loss of business. Quite often, the enforceability of a restrictive covenant is put into question following a termination. Sometimes they are deemed unenforceable because of consideration issues, or temporal length or breadth of scope. These issues can also easily be addressed through a mediation. It may also allow the employer to avoid a legal ruling that could suggest its similar contracts with all employees are unenforceable.

APPENDIX 2A

CHECKLIST FOR DEVELOPING AN INTERNAL WORKPLACE DISPUTE POLICY

1. Purpose

The policy should clearly set out the purpose and intent of the program to ensure the fair resolution of a range of workplace disputes that may arise in the course of an employment relationship. The policy should be fair in both reality and perception. It should be broad enough to encompass a wide array of workplace disputes.

2. Customize the Policy

The policy should be drafted with the particular organization and workforce in mind, which takes into account both the needs of the employer and employees. It should also be consistent with the applicable laws as well as the organization's corporate culture, mandate and vision. Accordingly, to be most effective at achieving its objectives, a policy should not merely be taken "off the shelf" for use by a particular organization. A customized package is important to ensure that it meets the needs of the employer and employees.

3. Wide Range of Options

The policy should set out a wide range of options to resolve disputes outside of the courtroom. These may include an open door policy, appeals to progressively higher levels of management, mediation and arbitration. The policy should clearly define each of the options and the processes to follow in each event so that they are clearly understood by employees and management.

4. Application of the Policy

The policy should clearly specify to which groups of employees the policy will apply. If any groups of employees (such as a certain level of management and above) are to be excluded, the policy should clearly indicate these exclusions. Some policies may also exclude new or probationary employees for a specified period of time. This does not mean that they are excluded from the application of human rights legislation. It may also exclude part-time or casual staff members. This determination will, of course, depend on the constitution of the workforce. As a general rule, all employees should be granted equal protection in terms of freedom from harassment and workplace disputes and no employees should be above these rules.

5. Nature of Claims to be Covered

Although it may be difficult at the time of drafting a policy to envision the nature of all disputes that may arise under the application of the policy, the policy should attempt to specify in general terms the kind of disputes that will be covered by the policy. Where certain kinds of disputes are to be exempt, these should be clearly outlined. Some employers may want the policy to be as broad as possible, while others may choose to exclude certain types of claims. By clearly outlining this, the employer can avoid misuse of the policy. The employer will want to avoid unnecessary and frivolous claims wherever possible. Providing guidelines may help to limit this potential abuse and misuse.

6. Procedures

In order to be effective, the policy must specify the precise procedures that are to be enforced by employees in filing their complaints. It may be helpful to develop complaint forms. Where there are time frames for filing such complaints, these should be clearly outlined in the policy. The procedures should be followed consistently by the company to ensure the fair and equitable application of the program. With respect to the workplace mediation and arbitration options, the policy should clearly specify how the selection of mediator/arbitrator as well as the scheduling and conduct of the mediation or arbitration shall take place. In the case of workplace mediations, the policy should try to delineate those circumstances where a neutral third party mediator should be used.

7. Cost Considerations

The policy should clearly specify what, if any, costs will be required by the employee as part of the process. If any amount of cost is to be borne by employees, the cost sharing should be fair, clearly delineated and applied consistently by the employer. In order to allow for wide and equitable application, costs would not normally be attributed to the employee (except possibly for the mediation and arbitration processes). However, it should be kept in mind that imposing some cost exposure to employees may help to limit abuse of the policy.

8. Notice of the Employee's Right to Counsel

The policy should provide that the employees have a right to retain counsel to represent them through any or all steps of the policy. However, representation should not be required or the policy may not have as wide an application as it is intended to have.

9. Provide for Fair and Adequate Discovery

The policy should provide for a fair and simple method by which the parties may obtain any information they require to support their case (within reason, bearing in mind the duties of confidentiality the employer may owe to other employees involved in the matter). The employee should be entitled to review his or her personnel file and should have access to all documentation contained therein. The policy should also provide for some sort of dispute mechanism for those instances where there is a disagreement with respect to the documentation to which an employee rightly has access in support of a complaint.

10. Right to File Other Complaints

The policy should state that the employee is not precluded from exercising his or her legal rights to file any other complaints or proceedings outside of the internal workplace grievance policy. The employee must always retain rights to the complaints through statutory bodies, as applicable. However, the policy may encourage employees to attempt to resolve the disputes through means of the policy prior to the commencement of other proceedings.

11. Notification

The policy should be clearly drafted in plain language wherever possible and all employees should receive a copy of the policy and be given an opportunity to fully understand the mechanics of the process. It may be helpful to provide in-house workshops to familiarize employees with the application of the policy. As with all important policies, employers are encouraged to obtain signed copies of the policy to ensure that employees have in fact read and understand the contents of the policy. The policy should also be posted at the employer's premises in visible locations.

12. No Reprisal

The policy should clearly state that employees will not be penalized in any manner for using the policy to deal with legitimate workplace issues.

Chapter 3
SETTING UP THE MEDIATION SESSION

Once a determination is made by at least one party to a dispute that mediation would be a worthwhile exercise, there are a number of issues to address and steps to undertake before setting foot in the mediation room. How do you approach the opponent? Who should act as the mediator? What style of mediation would be most beneficial and what format would be most effective? Where should the mediation take place?

Although these questions may appear straightforward, it is important that parties to a dispute maximize the benefits of the mediation process. In order to do so, each mediation session should be customized to meet the specific interests and needs of the parties.

The answers to these questions will depend partly on the particular characteristics of the parties and the complexity of the issues. It will also depend on the status of the relationship between the parties — that is, whether or not there is an existing employment relationship between the parties.

1. APPROACHING THE OTHER SIDE

The manner of the mediation and the timing of approaching the opponent were discussed in some detail in Chapter 2, "Determining When to Mediate", in the context of each of the factual scenarios. The next issue that arises is how to convince the opponent of the merits of mediation for the particular case in issue. The manner of approaching the other side will depend on the status of the dispute and the nature of your relationship with the opponent.

(a) Existing Employment Relationship

Where there is a dispute in the course of an existing employment relationship, the request or offer of mediation will normally come from one of the parties to the dispute. However, there may be occasions in an existing employment relationship where counsel will become directly involved at this preliminary stage. The suggestion may be made in writing or through telephone discussions. Typically, the underlying goal for both parties will be to preserve the employment relationship, and therefore, there is little danger in appearing weak or overly conciliatory by proposing mediation to the opponent. Where an internal process has been established in the workplace that provides for mediation, the party should follow the established procedure, unless due to the circumstances of the case, it is impracticable or inadvisable to do so.

(b) Terminated Employment Relationship

Where mediation is proposed as an alternative dispute resolution mechanism following the termination of an employment relationship, it is likely that counsel will be directly involved in carriage of the dispute and litigation may be ensuing. In jurisdictions where mandatory mediation exists, counsel will need to agree on which mediator will mediate the case and work together on scheduling dates for the mediation. However, in those jurisdictions without mandatory mediation, a different approach to scheduling may take place. In these cases, the proposal may be made in writing or by means of a telephone call from one counsel to another. Often, the proposal will be made by one counsel to another on a without-prejudice basis. Counsel may suggest mediation to the other and indicate that he or she would be prepared to canvass the possibility of mediation with his or her client if the opposing counsel would also undertake to do so. By proceeding in this manner, counsel is not prejudicing his or her client's interests or reducing the client's bargaining power by displaying an overwhelming eagerness to resolve the dispute.

Even if the request for mediation is made directly by one counsel to another, this should not normally be taken as a sign of weakness in the client's case. In most matters of litigation, both parties are willing to consider some process of resolution at some stage in the proceeding, regardless of their perceptions of the merits of their case. When mediation first started being used in employment law, this may have been a common perception, but that is no longer the case. In any event, by contemplating mediation, you as counsel are taking a responsible, cost-effective and ethical approach to the practice of law. If you are proposing mediation, you may wish to remind the opposing counsel of his or her "obligations" and the strong preference of the courts that mediation be considered by all parties to a dispute. A positive approach highlights the merits of mediation to an employment law dispute, and the fact that the process does not foreclose litigation may also be helpful in persuading the opposing counsel. If you are not successful in persuading the opponent of the benefits of mediation, it is likely that the pre-trial or case conference judge will recommend the mediation process to the parties, albeit at a fairly late stage in the proceeding. There are other positive steps that you as counsel may take in an effort to gain the agreement of your opponent to proceed to mediation. For instance, it may be helpful to assure your opponent that you will come to the table with all necessary decision-making authority and that you will be prepared to discuss certain specified issues in an effort to narrow the focus of the dispute. By doing so you may be successful at securing their agreement.[1]

2. SELECTING THE MEDIATOR

Once the parties have agreed to mediate a dispute, they must also endeavour to select an appropriate mediator and to determine the preferred style and format of the mediation. The parties must also resolve issues relating to the division of the costs of mediation. Sometimes, the parties will agree in principle to participate in a mediation but will make it conditional upon their reaching a satisfactory resolution on these and other important aspects of the mediation. In any event, unless the mediation is court mandated, any party can withdraw his or her consent to mediate for any reason, at least prior to signing an "agreement to mediate" with the mediator. We will discuss the significance of the "agreement to mediate" later in this chapter. If a party pulls out of a confirmed mediation, there will likely be a cancellation fee payable to the mediator by the defaulting party.

The task of selecting a mediator will normally lay with counsel, as the parties themselves will have limited knowledge of the mediation process and the skills and styles required of the mediator.

(a) Appropriate Background

Although one of the hallmarks of mediation is that it is presided over by an impartial, neutral third party, many counsel possess a personal list of preferred mediators. When counsel selects an arbitrator or adjudicator, it is not uncommon to assess the prospective candidate's political and social views by conducting a brief analysis of the candidate's reported decisions. One of the best indicators of the outcome of a decision-making process is to consider the decision-maker's history. The

---

[1] Appendix 3A is a sample letter.

prospective candidate's ideologies may be important in arbitrations and adjudications since the selected individual will have the full authority to make determinations on substantive issues. Accordingly, counsel will often make a determination as to whether the candidate is pro-employer/management or pro-union/employee. Counsel will often engage in a frustrating and time-consuming process of exchanging names of candidates with the opposing counsel until a mutually acceptable candidate can be found.

It would seem that this process of analysis would be less important when selecting a mediator as the mediator does not directly influence the outcome of the proceeding and is purported to be impartial and neutral. However, the reality is that when engaging in the process of selecting a mediator for an employment law dispute, there may still be a certain degree of classification that takes place by counsel along political and ideological lines. The mediator does exert some influence over the matter even though he or she has no decision-making authority. Where a mediator tells a litigant that he or she has a tough case to prove, the litigant may listen. Another consideration is how compassionate various mediators are perceived to be. In cases of discrimination, harassment and mental distress, plaintiff's counsel would likely prefer a compassionate mediator. The bottom line is that certain characteristics of a mediator may deem the mediator as either suitable or unsuitable for a particular case.

(b) Appropriate Experience

It is important to select a mediator who has the requisite degree of experience in dealing with the specific area of conflict. Where the matter involves uncomplicated issues of wrongful dismissal, most mediators will have a sufficient understanding of the issues and possess adequate experience in the area to allow them to preside over the mediation. However, where there are sensitive issues of sexual harassment, disability or other human rights issues, a mediator with specialized experience in the specific area of dispute may be required. Where there are complicated issues of compensation or contract interpretation, it may be important to select a mediator who has an expertise in dealing with complex employment law issues and who has an excellent understanding of the current case law in the particular area of the dispute.

You should also consider that there may be characteristics of the parties that will favour one mediator over another. Where the mediator will be performing some degree of evaluative mediation or where one or both of the parties need to be given a "reality check", the use of a retired judge or a very senior, experienced mediator may be preferred as they may be perceived by the parties as exerting an authoritative presence over the proceeding. Even though a retired judge has no actual authority to determine the issues in dispute, difficult parties may have greater respect for a retired judge than they would for any other mediator.

You may wish to request information from the prospective mediator about his or her experience, including the length of time he or she has been a mediator and the number of cases he or she has mediated in the particular conflict area. You may also request information relating to the mediator's success rate at resolving disputes in the particular subject area.

However, studies have shown that the quality of the mediator does not significantly impact the success rate of the mediation. Statistically, most mediators show about the same success rate. However, one study in the U.S. found that the quality of the mediator was a significant factor in how "successful" the mediation was rated by the parties, even though the objective criteria found equivalent success rates.[2]

Most of all, the selected mediator must inspire confidence and must have the ability to control the process (to the extent required, as in an ideal mediation the parties control the process) and guide the parties to a satisfactory resolution.

(c) Appropriate Training

For a worthwhile mediation, it is also important that the selected mediator possesses the appropriate training to conduct the mediation in the particular area of conflict. Counsel may ask a prospective mediator about his or her training credentials, especially where the case concerns special or sensitive issues including harassment, disability or discrimination. This may include asking the mediator how many hours of training he or she has completed in the particular subject area and what the training program included. Unlike family law mediators, there are no specific training requirements for those individuals representing themselves as mediators in the area of employment law, although most mediators will have taken substantial coursework in alternative dispute resolution processes. Although legal training is not essential, in most employment law mediations it would be beneficial. In some cases, it may be more important that the mediator possesses training and expertise in the subject area of employment law, rather than in the mediation process

---

[2] A.A. White, "Dispute Resolution Survey" (reported by Garcia J., in ADR, Houston, 1993).

itself. In these cases, a practising employment lawyer with a sideline practice in mediation or one who previously practiced employment law may be the most suitable candidate.

(d) Appropriate Methods and Style

It is important for you as counsel to keep in mind the particulars of the legal dispute and your client's specific needs and interests in evaluating what is the appropriate methodology and mediator style for the proposed mediation. The preferred methods and style used by the mediator are obviously tied to the mediator's experience and training. Many mediators will possess a broad and flexible focus. A good mediator will customize his or her approach to each case by taking into account the circumstances of the case, the characteristics of the parties and the specific directions of counsel. However, in selecting the appropriate mediator, you may consider the typical style, philosophy or strategies of the particular mediator in order to assess his or her appropriateness for the case. A retired judge may engage in a more evaluative process, which may be desirable for some cases. In addition, an evaluative mediator will likely authoritatively determine how the mediation will proceed. Other mediators may adopt a more "sensitive" approach which may be effective in resolving disputes involving emotional parties or difficult issues of discrimination, harassment or disability. A sensitive approach would also be helpful for a typical "workplace mediation" where conflict may exist between two or more employees. During the selection process, you may direct questions to the prospective mediators to determine their preferred approach as well as to assess their flexibility and adaptability. You may also request information from the prospective mediators with respect to their standard pre-mediation processes as well as what, if any, pre-mediation materials are required.

(e) Conflict of Interest Check

Before finalizing the selection, it is important for you to conduct a quick conflict of interest check to ensure that there are no conflicts with the proposed mediator and that the proposed mediator has no conflict with either of the parties. The mediator will need the names of the parties to ensure he or she has no conflict with any of the parties. Conflicts may include family, business or community relations, which may hinder the mediator's actual or perceived impartiality.

SETTING UP THE MEDIATION SESSION

(f) Fee Schedule and Availability

Two other important considerations that should not be overlooked in selecting a mediator are the mediator's fee schedule and availability. The fee schedule will be particularly important where cost is a substantial concern to either one or both of the parties. Some mediators may charge a minimum fee regardless of the length of the mediation session. Others may impose hefty cancellation fees unless sufficient advance notice of cancellation has been provided. Very experienced and hard sought after mediators may charge higher rates. Mediators with a specialized area of expertise may also charge premium rates. In addition, it is possible that the desired mediator may be booked solidly for a period of several months. Depending on the urgency of the matter, the mediator's lack of availability may be a significant drawback. You should also determine the estimated time required for the mediation session. Unlike other areas of law such as family law where several successive mediation sessions may be required, for most employment law disputes, only one session will be required. This session, however, may range from a one half-day session of two or three hours to two full days of mediation. If you are not sure how long a mediation will take, it is better to schedule it for a full day, or at least with an afternoon start time with the understanding that it may continue into the evening if necessary. If you select a half-day morning session, most mediators will have time restrictions as they may have another mediation scheduled for the afternoon. Having said that, many employment mediations can be easily completed in a half-day session. You should also keep in mind that there may be occasions where a mediation is suspended to allow the parties to either gather further information or consider settlement positions. The mediation session may then be reconvened at a future scheduled date. However, reconvening because you have run out of time is not always preferable because the parties will likely lose valuable momentum when they return to the mediation room at a later date.

(g) Selection Process

In a voluntary mediation, there is no established practice or rules or guidelines by which you must select a mutually agreeable mediator. Sometimes, counsel for both parties will have a candid discussion as to which mediators would be most suitable for assisting in the resolution of a particular dispute. Other times, one counsel may initiate the selection process by suggesting two or three mediators who he or she would consider acceptable for the case at hand. The opposing counsel may select one of the opponent's proposed candidates, or he or she may in turn propose alternative choices. This process may continue until a mutually agreeable mediator is determined. Sometimes this process is difficult and time-consuming as one or both counsel may be reluctant to easily concede to the opponent's suggestion, for legitimate or for merely strategic reasons.

Where you are unfamiliar with the mediators, it may be worthwhile to call colleagues who may offer names of suitable mediators while bearing in mind the nature of the dispute. A positive reference is often the best way to be assured that a mediator is effective.

In principle, agreeing to a suitable mediator should not be difficult. You and the opposing counsel do have a common goal of finding a mediator who can talk effectively to both sides and possesses enough insight and experience to be able to quickly understand the dispute, read the parties and assist the parties in finding a satisfactory resolution. In a specific practice area like employment law, most counsel will know the experienced mediators very well. It is sometimes difficult to come to an agreement as to who will mediate because those mediators favoured by employers are often not the same mediators favoured by employees. In addition, the circumstances of the case and characteristics of the parties might make some mediators preferable to one party over the other.

Prior to approaching the selected mediator, you should determine the manner in which the cost of the mediation will be divided or dealt with between the parties. In an employment law mediation, the company typically enjoys much deeper pockets than does the individual employee. Accordingly, sometimes the cost of the mediation will be paid entirely by the company. Most of the time, however, the cost will be evenly split. Some counsel argue that unless each party has a financial stake in the mediation by splitting the fees, there may be a reduced willingness on the part of the non-contributing party to make full use of the process as he or she will not be "out-of-pocket" for the cost of an unproductive mediation (except for his or her own counsel fees). It should be borne in mind that regardless of the understanding between the parties with respect to mediation fees, if the parties are successful at settling the matter through mediation, an alternative arrangement with respect to the payment of mediation fees may be reached as part of the overall settlement. Where the mediation takes place by virtue of an internal workplace policy, the company will often be responsible for all associated costs, except for a party's own legal fees, unless otherwise set out in the policy or as may be negotiated prior to the mediation session or as part of the settlement arrangement.

3. SETTING UP AN INFORMAL/INTERNAL "WORKPLACE MEDIATION"

The mediator selection criteria will likely differ where the mediation is conducted during the course of an existing employment relationship, rather than on a post-termination basis. Where the mediation is conducted pursuant to an internal workplace policy, the policy itself will likely delineate the process for setting up the mediation as well as the conduct of the mediation session. Where no such policy exists but a "workplace mediation" is to be attempted, the parties must determine who would be the most appropriate mediator, be it an in-house trained mediator, senior manager or third party mediator. Unless counsel is involved, the employer may make this selection on its own. Where the mediation is to be informal, the process of selection may be non-contentious and fairly straightforward between the parties, unless there is concern about a lack of impartiality, neutrality, objectivity or experience on the part of the prospective mediator candidates. Where the mediation is a workplace mediation, quite often a third party, external mediator will not be a lawyer but an individual who has received specialized training in dispute resolution processes. Some larger employers will have trained "neutrals" at the workplace to deal with matters as they arise. However, when the stakes are higher and there is the risk of bias or the issues are complicated, an external third party mediator would be preferred.

4. SETTING UP A COURT-MANDATED MEDIATION

Where a mediation is court-mandated, certain aspects of the selection process are predetermined and not within the control of the parties and their counsel. In the regions of Ontario where mandatory mediation exists, counsel have the option of selecting from an approved list of qualified mediators or selecting any other mutually agreed upon mediator. The mandatory mediation program started in Toronto and Ottawa in 1999 and in Windsor in late 2002. All employment law litigation matters are subject to mandatory mediation. The fee schedule relating to the mediation is determined by the *Rules of Civil Procedure*.[3] The rules also impose a deadline for the completion of the mediation.[4]

---

[3] R.R.O. 1990, Reg. 194.
[4] Rule 24.1.15(1).

The mediation must take place within 180 days after the first defence has been filed, unless otherwise agreed. If counsel are unable to agree on a mediator or they fail to do so by a specified date, the court will randomly select a mediator as well as the time and date for the mediation.[5] Most counsel would prefer to mutually agree on a mediator rather than rely on a roster mediator who may not be well versed and up-to-date on employment law. Where an employer insists on a roster mediator rather than selecting a mutually agreeable mediator, it is sometimes apparent that the employer has little or no intention of actually resolving the dispute at mediation but is simply "going through the motions".

5. SETTING UP A MEDIATION WITH THE HUMAN RIGHTS COMMISSION/TRIBUNAL OR OTHER ADMINISTRATIVE BODY

Where the matter involves a human rights complaint in Ontario, the parties are encouraged by the Human Rights Tribunal to consent to a mediation process that is conducted by a mediator of the tribunal. Typically, the mediators are vice-chairs of the tribunal who also adjudicate cases and are very experienced in mediation processes and knowledgeable about human rights legislation. Where a mediation is conducted through this mechanism, the parties do not have an opportunity to select the mediator. However, a mutually acceptable date for the mediation session is selected. There is no administrative fee attached to the mediation itself, although the parties may incur legal costs if they choose to be represented by counsel. There is no requirement for the parties to secure independent legal advice, although it is fairly common practice for counsel to be involved in the mediation process at the tribunal. Due to the often sensitive issues dealt with at this kind of mediation, it is quite common for one or more parties to be reluctant to confront his or her opponent in a face-to-face mediation. Sometimes, provisions are made to hold the mediation through a series of telephone calls, conference call or commonly, a mediation session where the parties are always seated in separate rooms. The conduct of a human rights mediation will be further outlined in Chapter 8, "Special Issues in Mediating Employment Law Disputes".

---

[5] Rule 24.1.09(6).

6. GENERAL MEDIATOR CHARACTERISTICS

Whether the mediation is conducted on an in-house basis or with a third party mediator, and regardless of whether it is a workplace mediation or post-employment litigation, both parties will demand and expect the following characteristics from the selected mediator:

- excellent communication skills
- skilled listener
- ability to focus on a goal of settlement
- ability to set aside biases and to be perceived as unbiased
- patience and ability to handle difficult, hostile and/or emotional people
- ability to be empathetic without taking sides
- ability to distinguish between stated positions and real interests
- thorough and articulate
- creative and flexible
- ability to secure and maintain the respect of both sides
- ability to digest, analyze and re-frame positions
- possess no stake in the outcome
- ability to control the pace and direction of the mediation
- ability to manage the interplay between the parties
- possess endless optimism that a resolution can be reached
- ability to take a practical approach and make practical suggestions towards resolution where appropriate

7. SELECTING THE LOCATION

Generally, the location of the mediation should be at a neutral site so that neither party feels or perceives that there is a "home advantage". The mediator may have access to an appropriate neutral site that includes a boardroom and at least one separate caucus room. On occasion, a party may feel that it is in their interest to hold the mediation in the opponent's territory as it is typically easier to walk out of someone else's office if the mediation is failing. For instance, this may apply where the employee senses that the employer has no legitimate interest in settling and is merely agreeing to mediate for ulterior motives, such as increasing the costs of the dispute. When this becomes evident, the employee may exert control by quickly ending the proceeding. On the other hand, an employee may be reluctant to hold a mediation at the opponent's office for fear that this will give the opponent an edge. Some terminated employees are reluctant to set foot in the employer's office or even that of the employer's counsel. Where the mediation is a workplace mediation, it is more likely that the mediation will take place at the employer's premises, although in some circumstances an off-site meeting would be strongly preferred. A determination of what is the appropriate location will, of course, depend on the particular circumstances of the case.

8. APPROACHING THE MEDIATOR

There are no hard and fast rules for approaching the mediator to set the mediation. Each mediator has his or her own approach. Some mediators will have their available dates posted online. Most will accept requests by email, voice mail or telephone call. Once a date has been secured, the mediator will usually set out the terms of the mediation in a letter to counsel. Setting up a workplace mediation is typically different and this will be addressed in a later chapter.

9. AGREEMENT TO MEDIATE

Most mediators provide a standard written agreement that outlines the terms of the mediation. The mediator will generally require the parties to a voluntary mediation to execute this agreement in advance of the scheduled date for mediation. The agreement to mediate should provide for the following items:

(a) confidentiality of all documents and discussions;

(b) fees, expenses, retainer, method and timing of payment and what, if any, fee is required for cancellation and the terms related to a cancellation;

(c) the right of the parties and the mediator to terminate the mediation session;

(d) the role of the mediator;

(e) confirmation that the mediator does not represent either side and that the parties have the right to independent legal advice;

(f) agreement of the parties to make full disclosure of all relevant facts and issues;

(g) confirmation that the mediator is not compellable as a witness in a court or other proceedings relating to the matter;

(h) agreement that the mediator may involve any necessary third parties in the mediation.[6]

---

[6] See Appendix 3B for a sample agreement to mediate.

It may be important to consider the legal significance of an agreement to mediate. Does it bind the parties to proceed through the mediation process? On occasion, a party may withdraw his or her consent to a voluntary mediation process prior to the date of the mediation. Typically, it is understood that either party may terminate the mediation at any time during the course of the process. From a legal perspective, it is arguable that the agreement to mediate should be upheld in the manner that any other agreement or contract would be upheld. However, practically speaking, if a party is no longer interested in participating in a voluntary mediation process, the chances of successfully reaching a resolution through this means will be substantially reduced and the exercise may therefore prove to be fruitless and a considerable waste of time and money. It should be kept in mind that where the mediation is mandatory, the parties may not have the option of withdrawing from the mediation process.

We have included a sample agreement to mediate for a workplace mediation. It is important to keep in mind that unless the resolution involves the payment of damages to resolve an internal dispute, the terms of the agreement will not likely be legally binding on the parties.

10. ROLE OF THE MEDIATOR

(a) Facilitative versus Evaluative Approach

As we have stated, the guiding principles of mediation are its inherent flexibility and adaptability. At the same time that the mediator is required to be a highly skilled individual who possesses specific experience, training and background, there is also a requirement that the mediator must allow for substantial flexibility and adaptability in his or her approach to each mediation session so that the proper process can always be fashioned to meet the parties' needs and interests. Although counsel may be drawn to a particular mediator because he or she is a proponent of one style of mediation over another, counsel should have some authority to mutually direct the style of mediation that will be most preferred and beneficial to a particular case. Counsel may determine this together in conjunction with the mediator.

In determining the best approach, one of the most important determinations for you as counsel to make is whether the mediator should play a purely facilitative role or an evaluative role in the mediation process. The two concepts are not mutually exclusive and it is generally considered that a mediation may be conducted anywhere along the facilitative/evaluative continuum.

Generally speaking, where a mediator plays a purely facilitative role, the mediator will focus on managing the discussions at the mediation to ensure that the process is as effective as possible. When a mediator adopts an evaluative role, the mediator will impose on the parties his or her opinions, views and expertise relating to the facts, issues and law involved in the dispute.

Where a facilitative approach is adopted, the parties will actively participate in the discussions, which will focus attention on the parties' needs and interests. The parties will be led into a process of narrowing the issues and formulating a mutually agreeable resolution. A substantial amount of the time, at least initially, may be spent in joint sessions where the parties will describe to the other side, their interpretation of the conflict as well as their wishes, needs, interests and rationales. Following these facilitative discussions, the parties may break apart so that settlement positions can be canvassed more thoroughly.

Where an evaluative mediation is desired, the mediator will provide an expert assessment of the technical or factual issues involved in the dispute. An evaluative mediator will often provide an assessment of the merits of each side's claim and the likely legal outcome if the matter proceeded to trial. The mediator will usually possess expertise and authority in the area of employment law gained through the practice of law or through judicial duties. Where an evaluative mediation is conducted, the mediator may require substantial written material from the parties in advance of the mediation session that sets out not only the legal and factual issues in dispute, but the parties' legal arguments. The mediator may also request each counsel to make brief opening statements highlighting the important facts and issues in the dispute.

Most employment law mediations fall somewhere in the middle of the facilitative/evaluative continuum, rather than at either end. Even where a mediator primarily uses a facilitative approach, he or she may use some aspects of the evaluative approach during caucus sessions when prompting each party to see the strengths and weaknesses of his or her case and when prompting each party to consider the consequences of not settling the dispute. With a facilitative approach, the mediator tactfully assists parties in evaluating their respective cases rather than imposing his or her opinions on the parties.

Where the matter is close to trial, a more evaluative approach to mediation may be preferred in order to make the best attempt at bringing the matter to a resolution. Obviously, a more interventionist approach to settlement may be necessary if the action has proceeded this far and both of the parties wish to resolve the dispute. An evaluative approach may also be preferred where parties require a "reality check" and are resistant to confronting the risks of continuing the case as well as appreciating the weaknesses of their case without a more invasive process.

You and the opposing counsel may expressly agree in advance of the mediation session, perhaps in consultation with the mediator, what approach should be utilized for a particular case. Alternatively, you may indirectly influence the mediator approach by selecting a mediator who generally adopts one approach over the other. Certainly, where counsel's preference is for an evaluative mediation, counsel should choose a mediator with expertise in employment law. Other times, you may wish to defer to the expertise of the mediator and allow the mediator to determine what would be the most effective approach, taking into account the circumstances of the case.

(b) Mediator Styles

Just as there are innumerable styles to "lawyering", there are many mediation styles. These styles need to be adapted to suit the interests of the parties and the dispute in question. In overseeing the mediation process, some mediators use a tough and invasive style that is sometimes referred to as "thrashing". Thrashing engages the mediator in a process of tearing apart each party's case by making them take a hard look at the strengths and weaknesses of their case. The mediator subsequently guides the parties in building their cases back up. Thrashing may be utilized by a mediator in appropriate cases in an effort to get the parties to consider realistic settlement figures. The "thrashing" typically takes place in caucuses and direct party communication is discouraged. Once one party has been "thrashed", the mediator will generally leave the party and his or her counsel alone to allow them an opportunity to confer, while the mediator proceeds in the same manner with the other side. Once both parties are at a point where they are prepared to consider more reasonable settlement positions, the mediator will work with the parties to reach an agreement.[7] This style involves many elements of an evaluative mediation and would be used most effectively in that type of mediation. It may be used effectively at any stage of litigation. It would be most useful on a post-termination mediation, rather than a mediation

---

[7] J. Alfini, "Thrasing, Bashing and Hashing it Out: Is This the End of 'Good' Mediation?" (1991), 19 Fla. St. U. L. Rev. 47 at pp. 66-73.

in the course of an existing employment relationship, as the process may not be particularly conducive to the preservation of good relations between the parties. The downside is that the parties may reach a resolution more as a result of fear and deflated confidence than through the usual mediation approach of cooperation and goodwill.

A related mediation style is referred to as "bashing". With this approach, the mediator focuses initially on the settlement positions that the parties propose at the outset of the mediation and engages in a process of attacking and bashing away at those initial positions in an attempt to get the parties to agree on a position somewhere in between the two divergent positions. Unlike "thrashing", the mediator spends very little time evaluating the merits of the cases. The obvious goal is to reach a quick settlement. With this approach, there is typically more time spent in joint sessions than with the "thrashing" technique but the overall session is usually shorter as an analysis of positions and interests is avoided. This is a technique that seems to be favoured by judges presiding over settlement or pre-trial conferences. It is perhaps most effective at a late stage in the litigation process and for obvious reasons, would not be preferred in the course of an existing employment relationship as the parties are unlikely to reach any agreement on the substantive issues of the dispute. Also, early in the litigation process, parties are not usually as willing to easily let go of their positions as they may be at a later stage. Rather, they merely agree on an outcome that they can both live with.[8]

A third mediator style is referred to as that of "hashing it out". This style emphasizes direct communication between the parties. The mediator takes a less directive approach and acts as a facilitator allowing the parties and counsel to speak directly with one another in forging an agreement.[9] This approach would be commonly used in informal workplace mediations to resolve workplace disputes, or any other dispute where there is an existing and salvageable employment relationship. This approach is less focused on reaching a fast resolution and places more attention on the particular needs and interests of the parties. Open communication is often a key element to reaching a satisfactory resolution in disputes of this nature. This would be the most commonly used mediator style for resolving internal employment law disputes.

---

[8] *Ibid.*
[9] *Ibid.*

11. CHECKLIST FOR SETTING UP A NON-MANDATORY MEDIATION

The following checklist may be helpful in setting up a mediation:

1. Determine the issues. Consider whether there is an existing employment relationship that the parties would like to salvage.
2. If there is an existing employment relationship, determine if there is an internal workplace policy.
3. Determine whether this is the appropriate time in the proceeding for the mediation.
4. Determine how the other side should be approached. By whom? Determine the method of communication. Determine how the request for mediation should be positioned.
5. Determine an appropriate mediator. Determine what background, experience and training are required to effectively mediate this matter.
6. Determine how the costs of the mediation are to be dealt with.
7. Determine when the mediation should take place. Is the matter urgent? Determine how long the mediation is expected to take. Determine where the mediation should take place.
8. Determine the role of the mediator. Determine the preferred style and format. Determine how to obtain the agreement of the opponent as to the selection of the mediator.

APPENDIX 3A

SAMPLE LETTER FROM EMPLOYEE TO EMPLOYER

Mr. Allan Grant
Human Resources Manager
ABC Co.
123 John Street
Anytown, ON
M4S 6Y7

Dear Mr. Grant:

As you are aware, I am very concerned about the negative performance review with which I was presented last month. I submitted written comments in response to the appraisal but my department manager has indicated that she is not prepared to change my performance rating.

In order to properly address these issues, which are of particular concern to me, I would be prepared to engage in an informal mediation process with the company. It is my view that these issues can be satisfactorily resolved if I am given an opportunity to voice my concerns.

Would you please advise whether such a process can be accommodated. I would be content if you were to oversee the proceeding between my department manager and myself. If you think it more appropriate, perhaps a neutral third party mediator could be considered.

I look forward to hearing from you.

Yours truly,
M. Brown

APPENDIX 3B

SAMPLE AGREEMENT TO MEDIATE (POST-EMPLOYMENT OR WHERE LITIGATION HAS ENSUED)

BETWEEN:

(Party)

- and -

(Party)

The parties named above have agreed to convene before a mediator for the purpose of attempting to settle the dispute between them through mediation. The parties hereby agree to the following terms:

1. Role of the Mediator

The parties acknowledge that the mediator is a neutral third party who represents neither party. The parties further acknowledge that the mediator is not a judge and will not provide a legal opinion or advice to either party with respect to any matters relating to the dispute or the mediation. The primary role of the mediator is to assist the parties to reach an amicable and consensual resolution of the issues in dispute.

2. Confidentiality

The parties agree that all communications between the parties and all documentation produced or disclosed through the mediation process, which are not otherwise discoverable, shall be communicated and/or disclosed on a without prejudice basis and shall be kept confidential between the parties. No such confidential communications and/or documentation shall be used in discovery, cross-examination, at trial, in this or any other proceeding, unless on the consent of the parties or pursuant to court order. The mediator cannot be called as a witness by either party and his notes and/or recollections cannot be subpoenaed in this or any other proceeding.

3. Liability

The parties acknowledge that the mediator shall not be liable for anything done or omitted with respect to the mediation and the mediator shall be granted the immunity that is granted to a judge under the *Courts of Justice Act*, R.S.O. 1990, c. C.43.

4. Full Authority to Settle

The parties acknowledge that they will bring to the mediation the individuals/company representatives who have full knowledge of the events in dispute and who have the full authority to settle. In the event such individuals cannot attend the mediation, the parties may ensure that such individuals are available by telephone or other means of communication, but only with the consent of both the other party and the mediator.

5. Independent Legal Representation

The parties acknowledge that the mediator will not give legal advice or a legal opinion. The parties acknowledge that the mediator has strongly encouraged that they each obtain independent legal advice with respect to the matters in dispute and that they are encouraged to attend the mediation session with their respective counsel.

6. Settlement Documentation

The parties acknowledge that either the parties themselves or their counsel will draft any and all settlement documentation or Minutes of Settlement and releases and that the mediator will not be responsible for so doing.

7. Cancellation of Mediation

The mediation has been scheduled for (*date*) at (*time*) and will be located at (*place*). The mediation session may be cancelled without penalty by either party on 48 hours' notice. If cancelled within 48 hours, a fee in the sum of $(*amount*) will be charged.

8. Termination of the Mediation

The parties understand that the mediator retains the discretion to terminate the mediation session at any time. The parties also have the right to terminate the mediation session, subject to any cost penalty as set out herein.

9. Costs of the Mediation

The fee for the mediator's services will be $(*amount*) per hour plus HST with a minimum of three hours. The mediator will charge for services at this rate for all time spent in connection with this matter including reviewing the parties' mediation materials, preparing for the mediation, telephone calls, meetings and the mediation session itself. Any disbursements charged by the mediator with respect to the matter will be charged in addition to the fees. The parties and/or their counsel are jointly and severally liable for the costs of the mediation.

Each of the parties and their counsel acknowledge that he or she has read this agreement to mediate and agrees to proceed with the mediation on the terms set out herein.

_____   _____

Party   Party

_____   _____

Counsel   Counsel

APPENDIX 3C

SAMPLE AGREEMENT TO MEDIATE (INTERNAL WORKPLACE MEDIATION)

BETWEEN:

(Party)

- and -

(Party)

The parties named above have agreed to participate in a workplace mediation in an effort to resolve issues that have arisen between the parties. The parties agree to the following terms:

1. The parties agree that the discussions taking place during the workplace mediation session and any agreement that is reached are without prejudice.
2. Any memorandum of understanding reached between the parties at the workplace mediation is not intended to be legally binding but represents an expression of interest of the parties. (Note: where damages are paid for an alleged breach, a release would be signed and this clause would be modified to reflect that the agreement is legally binding.)
3. The parties agree that:
    a) All relevant information to the issues must be disclosed and that all information disclosed will be confidential;
    b) A party to the workplace mediation can terminate the mediation at any time as the process is entirely voluntary.
    c) The mediator cannot be called as a witness in any potential legal action or claim that arises from this matter
    d) The mediator is a neutral third party and does not take sides in the matter or represent either of the parties.

Chapter 4

PREPARING YOUR CLIENT FOR MEDIATION

1. OVERVIEW

Proper preparation and organization are critical to the success of a mediation session. The process of preparation does not merely apply to counsel and the mediator, but also to the parties themselves. It is incumbent upon you as counsel to ensure that your client is properly prepared for the mediation session. In many respects, preparing a client for mediation is as important as preparing a client to provide evidence at an examination for discovery or trial. Even if no settlement is ultimately reached at the mediation session, the time spent in preparation for the mediation will usually be time well spent.

2. EXPLAINING THE MEDIATION PROCESS TO YOUR CLIENT

Some lawyers introduce the concept of mediation to their clients at their initial meeting when discussing the legal options that are available to the client in relation to the legal matter in question. Other lawyers introduce the concept of mediation to their client only once it becomes a real possibility for the case at hand. Obviously, your client requires this information in order to be in a position to provide his or her informed consent to proceed to mediation. Therefore, at the very least, you should ensure that your client has an understanding of the mediation process before he or she provides consent to a voluntary mediation. In the case of mandatory mediation, you will have an obligation to apprise your client of the process of mediation as a key legal step when determining whether to proceed with a legal action and addressing with your client the steps in the litigation process.

The onus is on you, as counsel, to ensure that your client understands the nature of the mediation process, the duration of the session, strategic concerns and what is expected of your client at the mediation session. The level of explanation required will, of course, depend on the past experience of your client and perhaps the sophistication of your client. Some clients, particularly representatives of employers, may have previous experience with the mediation process. However, you should never assume that because your client or corporate representative is an experienced businessperson, he or she will be a natural performer at mediation. All clients require adequate preparation to maximize the benefits of mediation.

The following general points should be highlighted in describing the mediation process to your client:

- the mediation process is non-binding
- agreeing to mediate does not commit the parties to settling the case
- the role of the mediator is that of a neutral third party who facilitates dialogue between the parties
- the mediator does not represent or favour one party over another
- the process is flexible and the parties control the outcome
- the parties typically play an active role in the mediation process
- the mediation requires a good faith effort on the part of the parties to discuss potential methods of resolving their dispute
- some compromise will typically be necessary to reach a settlement
- there will be a financial cost associated with mediation

In employment law disputes, it is not uncommon for an employee to feel an array of emotions from sadness and grief to anger and bitterness as they proceed through the legal matter. If you are acting for an employee, you should ensure that your client understands that the mediation process provides an opportunity to tell his or her story in a clear, concise and uninterrupted manner without fear that a display of emotion will negatively impact the case. Only in rare cases will you want to discourage your client from displaying emotion at a mediation session. This freedom of expression and degree of openness may not be possible (or advantageous) for your client when giving evidence at examinations for discovery and at trial where the parties are often more guarded and where the content and pace of the evidence tends to be controlled by counsel. The employer's representative will also be granted the right to tell the company's story. Although this representative is less likely to experience the range of emotion that an employee may feel, emotional outbursts do happen. Mediation is the one legal step that allows this unfettered emotion.

Your client should be aware of the confidential nature of the mediation process. In particular, your client should be aware that in the event the matter does not settle and the litigation proceeds, neither party can be held to any admissions, disclosures or concessions made at the mediation session.

Your client should be educated about how a typical mediation works. It should be explained to your client that pre-mediation materials are generally submitted to the mediator and are often exchanged with the opponent. These written submissions generally set out the facts, issues, strengths of the case, statement of damages and will often include a few critical documents that are being relied upon in support of your client's case.[1]

The client should be informed as to who will be in attendance at the mediation session. When you are acting for an employee, you should ensure that your client understands that a company representative will be in attendance at the mediation. Some employees will need to prepare themselves psychologically in order to confront a particular company representative face-to-face. It is often helpful for clients to visualize themselves at a mediation proceeding. You can assist by carefully explaining to your client the conduct of a typical mediation proceeding (although there certainly are some variances). This may alleviate some of your client's anxiety and apprehension about the process. It may even be helpful to describe to your client the likely layout of the room and the seating arrangements. Although each mediation process is unique, the following generic mediation process should be outlined to your client:

1. At the commencement of the session, the parties generally convene in a joint face-to-face session.

2. At the joint session, traditionally, each counsel will begin by making oral presentations about their clients' respective cases. (As will be discussed later, the newer trend has been to omit the opening statements and move right into the settlement discussions. Often, little time is spent in joint sessions.)

3. On many occasions, the clients are then given an opportunity to communicate their views of the case.

4. The process is unlike a hearing in that there is no formal evidence given and no formal line of questioning, although

---

[1] This will be further discussed in Chapter 5, "The Role of Counsel".

some questions may be directed to the parties by the mediator in order to elicit further information that may be of assistance to the mediator. The opposing counsel does not generally have the right to question your client directly.

5. No transcript or record of the proceeding is maintained.

6. As will be further described in Chapter 6, "The Mediation Process", other models of mediation are often used and if you are aware of the unique style of the selected mediator, you should advise your client accordingly.

7. You should advise your client that each mediation session is unique and the flexibility of the process and uncertainty of the outcome requires a level of spontaneity on the part of the parties and counsel.

8. A series of private sessions will typically follow the joint session (if any) in which the mediator meets separately with each party. In these private sessions, the mediator may ask questions in an effort to expose the strengths and weaknesses of each case. The mediator may ask each party in the private sessions about issues and positions the party does not want to disclose to the other side. Each party should be prepared to explore possible options for resolution with the mediator in these private sessions.

9. Your client should be prepared for long delays as the mediator may go back and forth from one side to the other in an effort to find common ground between the parties which may lead to a satisfactory resolution.

10. Your client should be prepared to make some tough decisions and concessions during the mediation and should be prepared to resolve the matter at the mediation session. Offers may only be on the table for the day of the mediation. Counsel should properly prepare clients for this as it may require a quick turnaround time on decision-making.

11. Your client should be prepared to be flexible and avoid being set in his or her positions. An open mind is more conducive to settlement.

You should prepare your client for the possibility that the mediator could spend several hours with the opponent and very little time with your client. There may be valid reasons for doing so, depending on the circumstances of the case. You should urge your client not to misinterpret these circumstances as favouritism. In fact, the mediator may be trying to break down the other side so that they appreciate the weaknesses in their case.

Your client should also be well prepared for frustrations, stresses and delays in the mediation process, as it often does not proceed as smoothly as desired. Where there are long lulls, you may find it very difficult to maintain a conversation with your client and to keep your client motivated and optimistic. You may find that your client's already elevated anxiety level increases during these delays. You should avoid using these delays as an opportunity to catch up on other files and return telephone calls or emails as this may create a perception of a lack of interest, both in the eyes of your client, as well as those of the mediator. If you feel it is necessary to conduct other business during these lulls, you should explain to your client in advance that you may use such lulls for this purpose and ensure that your client does not interpret this as a lack of interest. You should make your client aware that despite the best efforts of the parties, a resolution may not be reached through mediation. Your client should also be prepared for the possibility that even if a resolution is ultimately reached, there may be one or more stressful impasses before the matter is complete. The client should also be advised that typically, each party maintains the right to terminate a voluntary mediation session at any time if either one feels that the session is unproductive. Of course, in a court-mandated mediation, there may be a requirement to continue the mediation for a stipulated period of time, regardless of a party's perceived futility in the process. In Ontario, mandatory mediation is scheduled for three hours and the parties are encouraged to continue to work through the matter for the stipulated time.

3. DETERMINE WHETHER YOUR CLIENT REQUIRES REPRESENTATION

Depending on the nature and complexity of the dispute, it may be prudent to discuss with your client whether your attendance at the mediation session is in fact necessary. As discussed in Chapter 2, "Determining When to Mediate", there are many circumstances where counsel need not accompany a client to a mediation, and in some cases it may not even be desirable for counsel to attend, particularly where there is an existing employment relationship. Even where the employment relationship has terminated, there may be circumstances, although rare, where your client feels comfortable attending the mediation on his or her own. For instance, where the amount of damages in dispute is minimal, the issues are very simple and your client is cost conscious, your client may opt to attend the mediation without representation. This will more likely apply in a human rights mediation rather than in employment litigation. Before making this decision, it would be advisable to confirm who will be attending the mediation for the opponent. If you act for an employee and the company intends to bring its "big guns", regardless of the nature of the dispute, it may be advantageous for your client to also be represented. In addition, where litigation has been commenced, counsel should most certainly attend, unless the litigant chooses to be unrepresented in the lawsuit.

Practically speaking, this decision of attendance is only relevant for "workplace mediations" or human rights mediations. In making this decision, it is important that your client understands your role as counsel. Not only may you need to provide legal advice during the mediation, you may also be needed to act as a critical sounding board and provide necessary assurances to your client. It should also be kept in mind that your assistance may be important in closing the matter. Your attendance will also avoid unnecessary delays or impasses in the event your client chooses to seek your advice prior to finalizing a settlement. Furthermore, in the event the matter does not settle at mediation and proceeds to litigation, you and your client may be disadvantaged by your ignorance of what transpired at mediation if you were not in attendance. A mediation is also a good opportunity for counsel to assess the opponent as a potential witness. You should also bear in mind that as your client may be under extreme anxiety, particularly if he or she is unrepresented at mediation, he or she may neglect to address certain aspects of the claim. Where your client chooses to attend without representation, the process as explained to your client will differ somewhat from those cases where your client is represented. The basic tenets of the mediation process will remain the same. However, your client should be aware that he or she will be solely responsible for advocating his or her own interests. It should be made clear to your client that the mediator is not representing his or her interests and that the mediator's apparent kindness or compassion should not be mistaken for support for his or her case. As you will not be present to provide legal advice during the course of the mediation session, you should ensure that your client has a full understanding of his or her legal position. It may be helpful to confirm for your client the legal position and the strengths and weaknesses of the case through an opinion letter. It would also be prudent practice to confirm your client's decision to attend on his or her own in writing after discussing with you the pros and cons of so doing. Generally speaking, an individual who is attending a mediation session alone will require the same process of preparation as set out in this chapter. You would be well advised to spend considerable time with your client preparing for the mediation and offering the appropriate degree of coaching and guidance. In the vast majority of employment law cases, counsel does attend mediation sessions and accordingly, we will focus our attention in this book on preparing your client in this manner.

4. DISCUSSING LEGAL FEES

In preparing your client for the mediation and as part of the determination of whether your client will attend with or without representation, you should make it clear to your client what legal fees he or she is likely to incur during the mediation process. This will likely be of most concern to individual clients but it may also be an issue for some corporate clients who are working on tight litigation budgets. Notwithstanding the many cost benefits of mediation, your client should be aware that where the mediation does not finally resolve the dispute, it in essence adds one further step (and consequently one further outlay of fees) to the legal process. In most cases, a cost-benefit analysis will still deem the mediation session a worthwhile endeavour, even when taking into account the uncertainty of success. Even where no settlement is reached between the parties, there is often a lot to be gained from a mediation session. At the very least, the parties may narrow some of the issues in dispute and further, they may better appreciate some of the weaknesses in their respective cases, which might ultimately assist them in reaching a resolution. As mentioned previously, counsel can also do a quick assessment of the opponent as a potential witness (and also, an assessment of his or her own client as a witness) through participation in a mediation process.

5. DISCUSSING MEDIATION FEES

Not only should your client be fully apprised of the estimated amount of legal fees, he or she should be advised of the estimated fees associated with the mediator's services and, where applicable, the cost associated with the use of the facility where the mediation will take place. If you are acting for an employer in an employment law dispute, you should canvass the possibility that as part of the settlement, your client may be called upon by the other party to pay the full cost of the mediation as well as the legal fees for both sides. Although there is no requirement on the part of the employer to do so, this should be factored into the potential cost assessment for the employer, as it is a common practice in employment law disputes (and generally a good faith measure).

6. DETERMINING THE INVOLVEMENT OF YOUR CLIENT

Mediations are often more successful (or at least are perceived by the parties to be more successful) when the parties are actively involved in the mediation process. Where a party does not actively participate in the mediation process, or the party becomes a mere observer of the proceedings, he or she is unlikely to experience a high degree of satisfaction in the process. It is recognized that there may be limitations to the involvement of some clients due to their emotional state. As we will discuss in Chapter 6, "The Mediation Process", certain mediation styles/ models restrict direct party involvement. Certainly, in a "workplace mediation", the involvement of the parties is critical, especially where they are trying to work out terms for the continuation of, and improvement in the employment relationship.

The involvement of the parties in a mediation process is clearly distinguishable from their involvement in the litigation process. In the litigation process, you as counsel are responsible for actively representing your client's interests and eliciting the evidence in support of your client's case. Counsel are displayed "front and centre" in the litigation process. However, the underlying premise of the mediation process is that the parties themselves are the problem solvers as they are deemed to be in the best position to determine what is in their own best interest.

For many employees involved in employment law disputes, a mediation session will provide a therapeutic venue for venting their feelings and allowing themselves to be heard. Quite often, employment law disputes are not only about monetary damages, but also about hurt feelings, loss of self-esteem and the emotional upheaval that the individuals have been required to endure. Allowing employees to express themselves openly in a mediation session can be very cathartic and can allow the individuals to see the dispute in a more logical, clear and objective manner. Even when your client raises issues that you deem irrelevant, it could be helpful to canvass these issues in order to allow your client to clear his or her mind and advance to the next stage. Even though this may lengthen the mediation process and take the parties down extraneous paths, it may ultimately assist them in reaching a resolution. From an employer's perspective, there are also significant benefits in allowing a company representative to be heard and given an opportunity to explain the actions of the company. It may be especially helpful for the employee to hear this information directly from a company representative, rather than through the company's counsel. Often, your clients can express their interests and feelings in a more meaningful way than you, as counsel, can do on their behalf.

Accordingly, in a typical mediation, not only is it common practice, it is very worthwhile to actively involve your client in the mediation process by allowing your client to present the case in his or her own words. Although it is preferable and most effective if this is done somewhat candidly and without extensive coaching, your client should put his or her mind to this in advance of the mediation session. By addressing this with your client in at least a cursory manner in advance of the mediation, you can limit the risk that your client will say something that might later prejudice the case. Although statements made at mediation are considered confidential, practically speaking, there may be things that should be withheld from your opponent until the appropriate time.

You should also determine with your client what level of involvement he or she will have in the private sessions with the mediator. It is likely that the mediator will direct certain questions to your client during the private sessions in an effort to gain further insight into your client's case and to canvass settlement options. In most cases, parties should be encouraged to be as actively involved in the private session as possible. You should guide and direct your client to ensure that his or her position is in fact, communicated to the mediator in the manner intended. If your client is unresponsive to these questions, it could send the wrong message to the mediator. A client's display of emotions may cloud the issues or hinder communication and thus your involvement may be required. In rare cases where your client lacks the capability or confidence to answer these questions on his or her own, it may be in your client's best interest to limit his or her involvement.

7. PREPARING YOUR CLIENT FOR THE MEDIATION SESSION

After you have explained to your client the process of mediation and have determined what level of involvement your client will play in the mediation, it is imperative that you spend adequate time preparing your client for the conduct of the mediation session. The preparation of your client for mediation is similar to the process of preparing your client for examinations for discovery.

It is helpful to proceed as if you were preparing your client for a line of questioning. You should ask your client a number of probing questions, which touch upon all aspects of the case including any sensitive or weak points. You should assist your client in developing responses to critical questions that may be asked by the mediator. It may be helpful to conduct a mock mediation process. Your client should be familiar with all of the facts of the case, both those agreed upon between the parties and those that remain in dispute. You should ensure that you have obtained all documents in your client's possession that are relevant to the dispute. Your client should be familiar with all of the relevant documents, both those in your client's possession as well as those that have been produced in the process of litigation by the opponent. Where examinations for discovery have taken place prior to the mediation, you should ensure that your client takes the time to carefully review the transcripts of evidence of both parties. It is imperative that your client knows his or her case thoroughly and that any problem areas are carefully addressed. If it becomes evident at the mediation that your client does not understand his or her case, this can clearly hamper the mediation process and may also send the wrong message to the mediator and the opponent.

Through proper preparation, you should be successful at empowering your client to the extent that he or she can engage in the mediation process in an assertive and collaborative manner.

(a) Defining the Issues and Gathering the Facts

Before entering the mediation room, it is important that your client possesses a solid understanding of the legal and factual issues that are in dispute in the case. Your client should be capable of telling his or her story in an uninterrupted and unprompted manner. During the preparation sessions with your client, there may be additional facts that come to the surface which were not apparent during the initial consultations with your client. There may also be additional issues that developed during the litigation process. In the case of wrongful dismissal claims, some employees may appear to cope well with the loss of a job in the early stages but may later develop tremendous anxiety and distress as a result of financial stressors and/or their inability to obtain new employment. There are other unfortunate circumstances that can arise post-termination, including the onset of a disabling illness or condition. Other issues may develop as a result of the employer's conduct subsequent to a termination. For instance, the employer may provide false negative references to prospective employers which may unfairly hinder the individual's job search. In these circumstances, the new issues can be addressed in the ensuing litigation or mediation. Once a list of issues has been developed, counsel and client should carefully prioritize these issues, ranking them from the most important to the least important. You should assist your client in matching the relevant facts with each of these issues so that your client can develop a logical train of thought.

You should ensure that your client understands the facts as the law sees them. You should help your client understand that what matters most are not necessarily all of the facts, but the admissible evidence. Sometimes clients become sidetracked by facts or perceptions that are either inaccurate, unsubstantiated or cannot be proven. They often also get preoccupied with irrelevant facts and it is counsel's job to help them maintain their focus.

(b) Reviewing Strengths and Weaknesses

You should raise with your client both the strengths and weaknesses of his or her case. It is important to guide your client towards developing a level of objectivity about the case. Some clients may be reluctant to accept that there are weaknesses in their case and may require additional probing questions by you in order to elicit these problem areas. If you have not already made your client aware of the weaknesses in his or her case prior to this preparatory stage, now is the time to ensure that your client appreciates the deficiencies so that your client can maintain more realistic objectives leading into the mediation process. You should attempt to avoid a situation where these weaknesses are first exposed to your client by the mediator or the opponent at the mediation session. If your client is unprepared for this, it may certainly reduce any reasonable opportunities for settlement.

(c) Identifying Interests and Goals

One of the most important preparatory steps for your client is to identify his or her interests and goals as well as the perceived interests and goals of the opposing party. A substantial amount of time and effort at the mediation process will be devoted to exploring the parties' respective interests in an effort to blend these respective interests into a final resolution. It should be kept in mind that the interests that are identified by each party are unique to that individual. Although in most wrongful dismissal suits, the interests of the employee may include such things as compensation, benefits, re-employment, references and self-esteem among an array of other interests, there will be a wide variance with respect to how much weight and what priority a party will give to each interest.

You should spend sufficient time with your client identifying interests. In other words, you should determine what is driving your client in his or her claim or defence. Once these interests have been identified, you should engage in a process of prioritizing these interests. There may be one or two interests your client is simply not prepared to compromise on. Your client's objectives and goals should also be determined.

In preparing for mediation, you should also engage in a process of identifying the opponent's interests and goals. It is worthwhile to consider what may be the opponent's motivation in defending or pursuing the action, what the opponent likely wants out of the matter and why the case has not been settled thus far. By going through this exercise it may be possible to develop a better understanding of the dispute, which may better equip both yourself and your client to drive the matter to a resolution at the mediation session.

Through this process, it may become clear that not all of the parties' respective interests are divergent. Some of the interests that are identified may be common to both parties, or at the very least, one party may be indifferent to some of the issues raised by the other party. Where an option is in the best interest of both parties or is beneficial to one party and is not incompatible with the interests of the other party, this is referred to as "value creating". For example, an employee may be concerned about re-employment and thus interested in receiving relocation counselling. In many cases, an employer would share this interest. Where a move or option is contrary to the interests of both parties, it is referred to as "value destroying" and where it serves the interests of one party and is clearly against the other party's interests, it is referred to as "value claiming".[2] For instance, in many cases, negative publicity would be against the interests of both parties, but in some cases it may only be contrary to the company's interests. It could therefore be "value destroying" or "value claiming".

---

[2] Peter J. Bishop and Richard J. Moore, "The Role of Counsel in an ADR Process" (article contained in conference materials from "'Street Smarts' of Employment Law: A Workshop", Department of Continuing Legal Education, The Law Society of Upper Canada, June 6, 1996).

(d) Reviewing Settlement Options

As counsel, you should urge your client to maintain an open mind with respect to the dispute and to remain flexible when considering settlement options. It should be made clear to your client that mediation may allow for a broad range of potential remedies. In advance of the mediation session, it may be worthwhile exploring settlement options with your client. It is important for your client to consider non-monetary items, not just monetary ones. In employment law matters, a monetary settlement is often very important to an employee, especially where employment has been terminated and he or she is concerned about providing for the basic necessities of life. However, other non-monetary aspects of settlement may also be very important and your client may not consider these items without your input. When engaged in a dispute, all too often, the parties become focused on financial issues to the exclusion of all others. Even employers sometimes fail to consider the non-monetary aspects of settlement. It is most beneficial if your client's mind is opened to these possibilities long before you proceed to the mediation session.

Whether you are acting for an employee or an employer, a strategy should be developed that will enable your client to achieve the best outcome possible. A realistic settlement position should be determined in advance of the mediation, which may or may not conform to your client's initial expectations. Where you view your client's settlement expectations as unrealistic, you may need to perform a reality check on your client by directing your client to appreciate the weaknesses of the case. Clearly, it is at this time, in preparation for the mediation that you should address your client's unrealistic positions, hopes or expectations and try to understand your client's analysis of the case. It is important that your client understands that mediation is not the appropriate venue for tort reform and that if the client enters the mediation room with this objective, the session will likely prove to be very unproductive. You should also urge your client to consider alternatives to his or her settlement objectives and to gear his or her thinking to terms other than merely that of win/ loss. Your client should not enter the mediation room with the objective of "winning" as that is contrary to the basic tenets of the mediation process.

In determining realistic settlement positions, you should remind your client what the current law is with respect to the issues and what the likely outcome would be if the matter proceeded to trial. You should help your client understand that the result he or she achieves may not necessarily be what your client thinks is fair but merely what the law will permit.

Once a realistic settlement position is determined, you and your client should consider what the appropriate starting point for settlement will be. You should keep in mind that the mediator will likely attempt to cut each party's position down in an attempt to find some middle ground between them.

Your client should be encouraged to remain open-minded and to be prepared to continually reassess his or her settlement position as the mediation proceeds. Since mediation can serve as a pseudo-discovery process, it may become apparent during the mediation session that your client's case is either stronger or weaker than initially determined. In most cases, where a thorough pre-mediation preparation has taken place including the identification of interests, goals, strengths, weaknesses and settlement options, your client will have developed the necessary frame of mind to make a worthwhile and effective use of the mediation process.

(e) Determining Who Should Attend the Mediation

Quite often, in employment law disputes, individual parties will want to involve their spouse or other close relative in the mediation process. For some individuals, the accompaniment of a spouse or relative will be solely for the purpose of emotional support. However, because many employment law disputes involve the well-being and livelihood of the individual, which may substantially impact upon the entire family, the individual client may wish his or her spouse or relative to be involved in the decision-making process. In most cases, unless the attendance of this person is anticipated to be disruptive, their attendance should not be discouraged. In many cases, it can be very helpful as it may increase your client's emotional stability and level of comfort and confidence. It may make the mediation session run more smoothly. At times, it may be helpful to give the spouse or close relative the opportunity to speak at the mediation and express the impact that the dispute has had on their family, both from a financial and emotional perspective. However, what if a spouse's or relative's attendance at mediation proves to be disruptive or detrimental to your client's interests or to the conduct of the mediation? In these circumstances, it may make sense to suggest that the spouse or relative leave the session. Occasionally, there could be evidence or allegations to be presented by the employer at mediation that could prove embarrassing to the employee. It may need to be considered whether it is fair to present this information with a spouse or family member present.

Counsel should ensure that the individual client or company representative attending the mediation has the authority to settle the case. Where an individual client wishes his or her spouse to be involved in the decision-making process, then it would be most helpful to have that individual attend the mediation. Although it may be possible to reach your client's spouse by telephone during the mediation process, he or she will be at a disadvantage as the spouse will have missed the context of the discussions and negotiations. If your client wishes to involve his or her spouse or other individual in the mediation process, it is important that you adequately prepare this individual as well. He or she should be as knowledgeable about the process and the case as is your client. If this individual has not been adequately prepared, the individual may bring to the mediation his or her own biases or perceptions of the case which may scuttle the process. If this individual is also a decision-maker, then it is critical that he or she has been involved in all of the preparatory sessions along with your client. When you are acting for an employer, it is important that the company representative in attendance with you has the full authority to settle the file. It can be most inconvenient if the mediation reaches an impasse because the company cannot obtain proper instructions to settle on the terms proposed.[3] As counsel for the employee, it is worthwhile asking the employer's counsel who will be attending the mediation on behalf of the employer so that you can not only prepare your client but also satisfy yourself and your client that the most appropriate person with authority will be in attendance.

(f) Preparing Your Client for Uncertain Emotions

It is important that your client be emotionally prepared for the mediation session. Some mediations will proceed in a friendly, non-confrontational manner. However, in employment law, an individual's job performance is often questioned (even in a non-cause situation). In other cases, some unflattering personality characteristics may be raised by the employer. In cases of alleged harassment or discrimination, the victim may be emotionally fragile when asked to communicate his or her feelings or to address the nature of the allegations. In addition, the alleged accused may be subject to feelings of remorse, anger or sadness. Regardless of the nature of the dispute, in an employment law mediation, certain comments may be made that are personal or sensitive in nature. You should caution your clients to expect some resistance and hostility

---

[3] This aspect will be discussed in greater detail in Chapter 5, "The Role of Counsel".

from the other side and to remain calm, collected and dignified in the face of upsetting comments made by the other party.

8. CHECKLIST FOR PREPARING YOUR CLIENT FOR MEDIATION

1. Have you explained to your client what mediation is about?
2. Have you explained to your client the general mediation process?
3. Discuss confidential nature of mediation.
4. Discuss nature of client's involvement.
5. Discuss your role as counsel and role of mediator.
6. Discuss issue of representation.
7. Discuss legal fees and mediation fees.
8. Discuss whether spouse or other support individual should attend.
9. Determine issues and gather facts.
10. Assess strengths and weaknesses of both your client's case and that of your opponent.
11. Identify interests and goals.
12. Review settlement options.
13. Practice with line of questioning.
14. Conduct mock mediation session.
15. Highlight sensitive/weak areas and prepare client for uncertain and sometimes unexpected emotions.

APPENDIX 4A
CASE STUDIES

The following case examples may provide some guidance for you when preparing your client for mediation.

1. Cause Termination

Karen worked for ABC Office Equipment Ltd. for a period of five years in the position of sales manager. ABC was engaged in the business of the lease and sale of office equipment. The company terminated Karen's employment, purportedly for cause and alleged that she had sold a new photocopier to a customer at below cost value in exchange for repairs on her home. Karen denies the allegations and states that she did sell the product at below cost but maintains that she had discretion to do so. She states that she paid cash for the work completed on her home. Karen commenced a wrongful dismissal action against the company. The pleadings have been completed and the parties have agreed to attempt to mediate the matter prior to commencing examinations for discovery. The parties have agreed to exchange affidavit of documents but other than that, Karen and her counsel do not have a lot of information relating to the company's position of cause. In preparing for the mediation, Karen and her counsel attempt to identify the strengths and weaknesses of both Karen's case as well as that of the company, their respective interests and goals and potential settlement options. The strengths of the case include the testimony of the customer, the purported practice of the company in condoning below cost transactions and Karen's previous impeccable work record. The weaknesses include the fact that she did in fact sell the equipment at below cost and that she has no tangible proof that she paid for the repairs to her home. In addition, Karen feels that she has good contacts and may obtain a new job quite quickly which may limit her substantial claims for damages for reasonable notice and damages for loss of reputation. They have identified Karen's possible interests in priority sequence, as follows:

- compensation for damages for wrongful dismissal
- employee benefits
- good reputation
- fairness
- positive work record

- re-employability
- positive reference
- self-esteem
- legal costs
- anger
- revenge
- vindication

Karen and her counsel have identified the following potential interests of ABC:

- compensation paid to Karen
- management accountability
- customer relations/satisfaction
- productivity
- ensuring compliance with policies
- avoidance of setting precedent
- morale
- public image
- legal costs
- avoidance of negative publicity

Karen and her counsel developed a variety of settlement options. They were then able to develop a strategy and plan for the negotiation process at the mediation session and determined both their starting settlement position and their bottom line settlement position.

2. Sexual Harassment

Jane worked as an executive assistant for a senior vice-president of Ultra Consultants Inc. From the commencement of her employment, Jane felt very uncomfortable being alone in the office with her boss but was not certain why she experienced this sense of uneasiness. When he spoke to her, his eyes were focussed on her body. Jane became increasingly uncomfortable. One evening when Jane stayed late to finish typing a report, her boss walked up behind her and began massaging her neck and shoulders. Jane felt very uncomfortable and immediately asked him to stop touching her. The following day, Jane noticed a distinct change in the manner in which her boss talked to her. He became very critical of her performance and she began to fear the loss of her job for cause. Jane was suffering a lot of stress and anxiety and began to doubt whether she should have confronted her boss in the manner she did. Jane did not feel that she could continue working in this arrangement and knew there were no other appropriate positions for her within the company. She ultimately hoped to leave the company with a satisfactory severance package. Jane filed a complaint of sexual harassment and retained counsel to assist her with the matter. The parties are preparing for a mediation and Jane has decided that she would like independent counsel present. In preparing for the mediation, Jane and her counsel identified the following strengths in her case: positive performance to the date of the rejection; boss's conduct has the appearance of reprisal; no tangible evidence that the criticisms were warranted. They also identified the following weaknesses: no witnesses; short term of employment; boss yields a lot of power in the organization.

Jane and her counsel identified her interests as follows:

- self-esteem
- self-worth
- self-doubt
- safety
- emotional stability
- comfort in her working environment
- compensation

They identified the following as potential interests of the company:

- productivity
- morale
- safety and well-being of employees
- avoidance of liability
- avoidance of publicity

They also identified the following as potential interests of her boss:

- fear of penalty or job loss
- reputation
- avoidance of publicity
- avoidance of personal liability
- anger
- avoidance of further embarrassment

Jane and her counsel developed a number of settlement options which included moving to a position in a different department, a generous severance package for Jane (which would appropriately compensate her for the improper actions) or transferring her boss to another area. Jane and her counsel also developed a negotiation strategy they hoped would achieve her preferred settlement option of receiving a severance package.

Chapter 5
THE ROLE OF COUNSEL

1. OVERVIEW

As counsel in an employment law mediation, you will typically wear a number of different hats. Your role may include that of coach/counsellor, communicator, protector, educator, monitor and strategist. Your level of involvement in a mediation session will depend on a number of factors, most importantly, the particular characteristics of your client and the nature of the dispute. As counsel, not only must you take the proper steps to prepare your client for a mediation session, but you must also take the necessary measures to ensure that you are well prepared for the session, which will allow you to most effectively represent your client's interests.

2. DETERMINING YOUR ROLE

One of the defining principles of mediation is that the parties themselves are the ultimate problem solvers. The parties are given an opportunity to tell their story in their own words. Through their involvement, they become empowered to the extent that they can exert greater control over the process and ultimately, the outcome of the mediation session. Generally speaking, as counsel, your role at a mediation session is not to make judgement calls or impose views on your client. Your primary role is to help your client develop and choose a resolution that is best suited to your client. Obviously, some clients will need a lot more assistance than others in developing these settlement options. Although you have been retained as an advocate of your client's interests, you should refrain from taking control over the mediation process. The risk associated with controlling the process is that the focus of the mediation session may change to a determination of legal rights and issues rather than a determination of the client's needs and interests. This may result in a loss of valuable time at mediation, stalled proceedings and ultimately an unsuccessful outcome. You should avoid turning the mediation into an examination for discovery or a trial. You should remember that mediation requires a different set of skills than those required in the litigation process. An experienced litigator may not necessarily be skilled at mediation. By using the same techniques and skills that you use in litigation, you may actually be doing your client a great disservice. In many cases, an overly aggressive or antagonistic approach on the part of counsel may be detrimental to the mediation process.

Even though the parties are expected to drive the mediation process that does not imply that your role as counsel is unimportant. Where you do attend with your client at a mediation session, you may offer unique skills and experience that will greatly assist your client in achieving his or her objectives and reaching a satisfactory resolution.

Unfortunately, due to the sensitive nature of many employment law cases, facts and evidence are often disclosed that may be upsetting to some individual clients. As a result, like it or not, one of your primary roles as an employment lawyer is to act as a coach and pseudo-counsellor/therapist to your client. This role, although common in the practice of employment law, is often most in demand at a mediation session. If your client becomes emotionally upset by matters raised at the mediation, you may be required to lend a compassionate ear. It will also be incumbent upon you to tactfully and delicately redirect your client's attention to the issues that are in dispute and to the goals of achieving an acceptable resolution. These skills will flow naturally for some lawyers and for those lawyers to whom they do not, appropriate skills building may be helpful in order to effectively represent your client at a mediation session.

You will also be required to act as a strong communicator. This is more akin to the traditional skills required of a lawyer. Since your client may be uneasy, nervous or agitated throughout the mediation process, you may be required to skilfully communicate your client's interests in a compelling and persuasive manner. Because you are not personally involved in the matter, you will typically be in a better position to provide a less impassioned communication of the case than your client will typically be capable of providing.

It is also incumbent upon you to act as your client's strategist. Although settlement strategies and positions will be developed in conjunction with your client prior to the mediation, the process of strategizing and reassessing your position must continue throughout the mediation session. As all lawyers are sadly aware, legal matters often do not proceed in the manner anticipated or planned. However, by utilizing your skills of analysis and assessment throughout the mediation session, you will be able to continually help generate resolution options to your client's advantage. You must also encourage your client to maintain an open mind throughout the mediation process and to remain flexible in the face of unexpected circumstances.

You will also be responsible for acting as a protector of your client. One of your primary roles at a mediation session will be to ensure that your client is not being unfairly taken advantage of or "bulldozed" into a less than satisfactory resolution. Where you are acting for an individual client, it is not uncommon for your client to feel intimidated, especially where the company brings out its "big guns". Through your involvement or mere presence, you can ensure that the process maintains some stability and a more "even playing field".

You may also perform the important role of educator during the mediation process. Although mediators will generally discourage counsel from providing extensive legal analysis and arguments, as these are better left for the courtrooms, there are times when you may be required to provide a legal analysis of the case on your client's behalf. In an evaluative mediation, you may be called upon to provide greater legal analysis than you would provide during a facilitative mediation.

As a general rule, you will be expected to remain reasonable, calm and confident throughout the mediation process. Even where your client becomes angry, emotional or upset, you may exert greater influence by simply remaining calm at the centre of the storm. In essence, you must be a bit of a chameleon and utilize your skills as required through the often unpredictable and sometimes tumultuous mediation process.

3. PREPARATION OF MEDIATION MATERIALS

Most mediators will require the submission of pre-mediation materials so that they can effectively understand the issues and problems at hand in advance of the mediation session. It also allows them an opportunity to ponder what they will need to do in order to facilitate a settlement of the case. Some mediators will be very specific as to what form of materials they require. You would be well advised to inquire of the mediator what he or she expects in terms of pre-mediation materials and what deadlines for such submissions have been imposed. Where the mediation is a mandatory mediation, the form of the materials is stipulated although many counsel will adapt the prescribed form slightly to best suit their case. Where cost is a concern to you and your client, the extent of materials required by a particular mediator may be an important criterion in your selection process.

MEDIATING EMPLOYMENT DISPUTES

Generally speaking, mediators will require a statement of the legal and factual issues in dispute in the matter as well as a statement by each party of his or her case, without substantial legal arguments. In your written materials, you may briefly state your perspective of your client's case and the basis for your evaluation. A common error on the part of lawyers is to provide more information than is required. This can be particularly disruptive of the mediation process. You should be careful not to burden the mediator with unnecessary details and facts. It is important that you isolate the important from the extraneous items and proceed to succinctly present only the most cogent facts in your materials. It is usually helpful to also include copies of the most important documents in your pre-mediation materials, but you should avoid overwhelming the mediator with unnecessary or only marginally relevant documents. Since inherently, the mediation process avoids a determination of legal issues, a large number of documents may bog down the parties into a process more akin to discoveries which may consequently, obstruct the effective use of the mediation session. Where litigation has been commenced, a copy of the pleadings should be included for the mediator's review. Similarly, where the dispute involves a human rights, employment standards or other statutory complaint, a copy of the applicable complaint and response should be provided.

It is the practice of some counsel, although probably rare, to avoid sharing their mediation materials with the opposing counsel. If there is a disagreement on this point, you may seek some direction from the mediator as to what his or her expectations are with respect to the exchange of materials. As long as no confidential documents or information is being disclosed through the mediation materials which you are not willing to present to the other side, there seems no valid reason to withhold the documentation from the opponent. Presumably, if litigation has been commenced, you will be required to provide full documentary disclosure to the opponent. Therefore, there seems little merit in refraining from sharing this information through the mediation process. Even if the case has not proceeded to litigation, it is often preferable to exchange this information, as the parties may be clearly disadvantaged if they have little or no understanding of their opponent's case. In a mandatory mediation in Ontario, each counsel is required to present a copy of the mediation brief to the opposing counsel.

In fact, when the parties have each disclosed to their opponent their analysis of the facts and issues, the mediation process may be shortened. On the other hand, if both parties walk into the mediation session with little or no information or documentation from their opponent, a lot of time may be wasted at the mediation session discussing these preliminary issues and background information. For instance, where an employee has been terminated for cause, failure to share the reasons for termination prior to the mediation may place the employee and his or her counsel at a substantial disadvantage. Similarly, a mediation held to resolve issues of sexual harassment may be stalled where the complainant and alleged accused only become informed of the status of the investigation at the commencement of the mediation.

Where a dispute involves issues of disability, the production of relevant medical documentation may be vital to a satisfactory resolution. The failure of the parties to exchange information may create unnecessary impasses which would not be in the interest of either party. Although a clear determination of legal issues is generally avoided at a mediation, the parties will be disadvantaged if they are forced to negotiate their interests in a vacuum. To avoid these potential problems, you should ensure that your opponent has produced whatever documentation you deem relevant well in advance of the scheduled mediation session.

If there are facts that you wish to refrain from sharing with the other side but are willing to disclose to the mediator, you may simply add a confidential attachment to the materials forwarded to the mediator. To avoid any confusion, it is important to clearly indicate to the mediator that you do not wish the other side to have knowledge of those particular facts and you should state your reasons for withholding that information.

In Ontario, there are specific stipulations with respect to mediation materials required for all mandatory mediations.[1]

4. SELECTING YOUR CLIENT REPRESENTATIVE

If you are representing a corporate client in a mediation, it is important that you carefully select the most appropriate person to represent the company's interests at the mediation session and to provide you with instructions. Unlike an examination for discovery, the employee (or plaintiff) will generally not have a right to dictate who is to represent the company. It should be noted, however, that it may be important to an employee that a particular representative of the company attend and this may even be expressed as a condition of mediation. It may be that the employee wishes to confront a particular individual, be it a former manager or other representative. It is also possible that the employee and his or her lawyer want to ensure that the representative who attends the

---

[1] See Appendices 5A and 5B.

mediation has sufficient authority to settle in order to ensure a meaningful and worthwhile mediation process. Ideally, as corporate counsel, you should ensure that the attending company representative has full authority to settle the case. You should carefully canvass the list of prospective corporate attendees. The representative who is selected must not only have proper settlement authority, but must also be very familiar with the case. If the ultimate decision-maker is not available to attend, it is sometimes permissible to seek instructions by telephone. However, this approach raises some concerns. Not only does it give the impression to the plaintiff and his or her lawyer that the matter is not of importance to the company, which can negatively impact the outcome, but it may also be difficult to obtain proper instructions where the decision-maker has missed the full context of the discussions that have taken place during the mediation session. The decision-maker may be provided with only an executive summary of the discussions as well as the settlement proposal, and will have missed all of the discussions and analysis leading up to that point. The company may have set a notional bottom line position in advance of the mediation and without the benefit of direct involvement in the mediation the decision-maker may be unwilling to surpass that bottom line position.

However, even the most informed representative may not be the most appropriate attendee where he or she is emotionally or personally involved in the case. Although it is generally acceptable for an employee in an employment mediation to display emotions, it is usually not productive for the company's representative to become overtly emotional during the mediation process. That is not to suggest that the company representative should be devoid of emotions. However, it is normally most effective and productive if the company's representative maintains a certain degree of personal detachment from the issues in dispute and a calm demeanour throughout the mediation process. After all, they are representing the company's interests, not their own (with the exception of those cases where the company representative is also a personal defendant in the case).

On many occasions, more than one company representative will attend a mediation. The general rule is that if multiple representatives are felt to be important to the success of the mediation, they should be permitted to attend. However, the plaintiff and his or her lawyer need to be satisfied that there is a legitimate reason for the attendance of additional representatives. The attendance of multiple representatives could negatively impact upon the ability of the parties to resolve the dispute, as the teams will be unbalanced. A full "team" on the employer's side may be unfairly intimidating to the employee. Where this becomes a problem, the mediation process could be restructured so that more time is spent in private sessions where the plaintiff may experience a greater comfort level in the absence of the opponent.

5. PREPARATION OF YOUR OPENING STATEMENT

Although the mediation process generally maximizes client involvement, there is still plenty of opportunity for you as counsel to utilize your well-honed skills and be involved in the presentation of your client's case. In addition to the submission of written materials, you may have an opportunity to verbally present your client's case at the opening of the mediation session. Although traditionally, most mediation sessions commenced with opening statements during the "public" session of the mediation, this step has started to fall out of favour. The feeling is that when faced with short time frames for the mediation session, there is little point in spending much time summarizing what is already set out in each party's written briefs. Instead, parties may convene but conduct that public session as a joint fact finding session. Counsel will jointly decide in conjunction with the mediator whether opening statements will be given.

Where given, the opening statement should not simply be a regurgitation of what is contained in the written materials. The opening statement should succinctly and effectively highlight the key elements of your client's case. It is not unlike an opening statement given at the commencement of a trial, although it will typically be a more informal presentation. The presentation should be concise and persuasive and you should endeavour to capture the other side's attention. The opening statement that you give may set the tone for the entire mediation session. Accordingly, the tone should be positive. Aggressive statements, threats and complaints which may deter settlement discussions should be avoided. However, you should be clear in your presentation by stating or reminding the opponent of your client's interests. It is important to remember that the purpose of the mediation session is to facilitate settlement discussions and, therefore, the tone may be very important to the outcome of the mediation.

In order to be most effective, throughout your opening statement, you should address not only the mediator but also the opposing counsel and the opposing party. Establishing eye contact may be very important in setting the stage for an effective mediation. This is of course distinguishable from the approach at trial (at least a non-jury trial) where counsel always addresses the judge in his or her opening statements rather that the opposing counsel or the parties themselves. It is important that you attempt to humanize both yourself and your client for the benefit of both the opponent and the mediator, as this may allow a positive connection with the other side. If you are acting for an employer, you should allow yourself to express some degree of sympathy and compassion, without acknowledging responsibility for the company's alleged actions. This element of humanization may be useful in the mediation process only and counsel may take quite a different approach should the matter proceed further through litigation.

In some cases, it may be effective to allow your client to deliver part of the opening statement. This will obviously depend not only on the comfort level, confidence and abilities of your client but also on the nature of the dispute. Some mediators may encourage the parties to participate in the opening statements. In employment law disputes, client involvement is often very worthwhile, not only for purposes of enhancing resolution possibilities, but also for the therapeutic value it may bring to the parties themselves.

6. PREPARATION OF THIRD PARTY STATEMENTS

In some cases, it may be worthwhile to obtain written statements from third parties prior to the mediation session. Third parties will not normally be present at the mediation session (aside from family members or spouses who attend with the parties as discussed in Chapter 4, "Preparing Your Client for Mediation"). These third party statements may be helpful for refuting the positions of your opponent or for demonstrating to your opponent what the evidence of certain witnesses will be in the event the matter proceeds to trial. If the mediation is proceeding smoothly, it may not be necessary to refer to the third party statements. However, they can prove to be useful where the mediation reaches an impasse because of a dispute over certain evidence or the expected nature of witness testimony. In addition, where an investigation has been conducted that has resulted in the termination of employment or other disciplinary measure, the investigation report should be available and open to be scrutinized. This may give the mediator additional tools to use in resolving the dispute as it may assist the parties in appreciating the strengths and weaknesses of their respective cases.

7. PREPARATION FOR PRIVATE SESSIONS

Typically, a mediation will include both public and private sessions. It is not only during the joint or public session that you will be required to make verbal presentations. In private sessions, you and your client will have the unique opportunity to candidly discuss the strengths and weaknesses of your client's case with the mediator alone. In preparation for the mediation session, you should consider what presentations you would like to make privately to the mediator. By sharing certain points with the mediator privately, the mediator may be able to more effectively assist the parties in resolving the case. It is at this time that you may want to disclose to the mediator certain facts or privileged documents that you wish to withhold from the other side. There may be occasions where you feel that it is in your client's interest to withhold certain information even from the mediator. As a general rule, it is often preferable to disclose all information to the mediator because it is sometimes difficult to assess on your own (without knowing the position of the opponent) what information might be the key to bringing the matter to a satisfactory resolution. Rather than withholding this information, it is often best to share it with the mediator and decide jointly with the mediator what should be shared and what should be withheld from the other side. Where key points of evidence are withheld, the mediation process may be stalled which can lead to a needless waste of time, money and resources. Of course, it goes without saying that parties must comply with all disclosure requirements as part of the litigation process.

8. NEGOTIATION STRATEGIES

At mediation, you as counsel will play an important role in the negotiation process that forms a significant aspect of the mediation process. There are numerous approaches to negotiation and you should be familiar with the various approaches and ensure that the most effective approach is used to serve your client's particular interests.

(a) Positional Bargaining

The traditional approach to negotiation is commonly known as positional bargaining. It is adversarial in nature and is characterized by the parties making extreme opening statements and attempting to persuade the opponent of the merits of their case (sometimes through intimidation). The parties gradually move closer together through a series of incremental concessions until a final agreement of compromise is reached. Positional bargaining may be effective where the settlement is merely a matter of money and where the parties are not anticipating a future relationship. The bluffs, tricks and aggressive positions used in this approach may preclude the salvaging and continuation of an employment relationship and it is therefore not recommended for use during a "workplace mediation". A major drawback of this approach is that it may cause the parties to overlook other needs and interests, particularly when they are not placed on the table at the outset of the mediation.

(b)   Collaborative Negotiation

Collaborative negotiation is less competitive and adversarial in nature than the traditional positional approach to bargaining. The focus of this form of negotiation is to go beneath the initial positional claims in order to uncover the real needs and interests of the parties. Typically, the dispute becomes larger than just one issue and it becomes a determination of multiple issues. Even in a simple wrongful dismissal dispute, there may be much more involved in the dispute than a determination of the amount of reasonable notice. These may include simple items such as obtaining a letter of reference as well as the structure and timing of the payment. This form of negotiation generally allows for more creative solutions to the dispute than do other methods of negotiation. This approach can be very effective where the parties are hoping to salvage an employment relationship during a "workplace mediation" but it can also be very effective during a post-employment mediation (with or without litigation).

(c)   Interest-based Negotiation

The goal of interest-based negotiation is to meet the legitimate interests of each side and resolve the conflict in a fair manner. This approach was developed by R. Fisher and W. Ury.[2] One of the defining features of this approach is separating the people from the problem by acknowledging the other party's feelings and treating them with respect, without necessarily conceding on the substantial points. The second feature is that the parties focus on the needs and interests that underlie their positions, rather than focusing on the positions themselves. Often, the underlying interests are easier to negotiate than are the positions. The

---

[2]   *Getting to Yes: Negotiating An Agreement Without Giving In*, rev. ed. (Markham: Penguin Books, 1992).

third feature is that the parties are encouraged to consider a wide range of options before reaching a settlement. The goal is to select those settlement options that will satisfy the interests of both parties. The final defining characteristic is that negotiation should occur independently of the desires of the parties and should be based on objective criteria. This approach has gained wide recognition and respect and is commonly used in the mediation of employment law matters. This approach to negotiation truly goes hand-in-hand with the fundamental aspects of mediation. It certainly has the benefit of ending the matter on positive terms, regardless of whether or not there is a continuing employment relationship.

9. PREPARATION OF DRAFT SETTLEMENT AGREEMENT

At the commencement of a mediation session, you may have no idea whether the matter will settle and, if so, on what terms. Even so, there are certain generic terms that can be expected in the event of the settlement of an employment law dispute. You may wish to draft standard minutes of settlement in advance of the mediation session. Although the mediator may have standard, "boilerplate" minutes of settlement available for your use at the mediation, you may wish to customize the settlement documentation to suit the dispute in question. The mediator's form of documentation may not be appropriate for an employment law matter, particularly where the mediator operates a general mediation practice. Although counsel for each party may prepare draft settlement documentation, it is more likely the plaintiff's counsel who will initiate the drafting process. However, the defendant's counsel will definitely want to have a hand in drafting the release language as it will form a critical part of any settlement agreement.

Once a settlement has been reached at the end of a long mediation session, the participants will be tired and would probably prefer to conclude the session rather than belabour over the specific wording of the minutes of settlement. If the process of developing the minutes of settlement is difficult or time consuming, there is a risk that the agreement reached in principle may fall apart before the minutes are actually signed. Therefore, there are substantial benefits to ensuring the fast and uncomplicated completion of the documentation. When drafting under these pressing conditions, it is easy to forget certain standard but important clauses. There are several boilerplate clauses that can be very important to the company in employment law settlements including confidentiality of the terms of settlement, confidentiality of employer information as well as standard release clauses, which include a full release of the applicable employment statutes. In addition, an indemnification clause for income tax implications and employment insurance may be important, depending on the structure of the settlement and the status of the employee's employment insurance claim. A pre-prepared draft settlement agreement can limit the margin for error and make the finalization of the documentation at the mediation session a less onerous task. This draft can then be modified as required at the time of settlement. The benefit is that the parties will be less likely to miss key points.

10. AVOIDING COMMON PITFALLS

What you do as counsel at an employment mediation session can have a substantial impact on the outcome of your client's case. It is, therefore, important that you avoid common pitfalls to ensure that your client is receiving the best legal service possible. The following list highlights some things that you should keep in mind throughout the mediation process:

- Where opening statements are given, avoid making them overly aggressive or inflammatory as this may be counterproductive. Instead, save any such statements for the private caucus sessions. However, there may be occasions when such grandiose statements are appropriate. Do your best to assess whether this is one of those occasions.
- Ensure that the proper parties are in attendance at the mediation session, both your own and those of your opponent.
- Ensure that the persons in attendance have sufficient authority to settle the matter as the mediation will be most effective when the mediator has an opportunity to meet face-to-face with the decision-maker(s) for each party. The mediation will likely proceed with fewer interruptions and impasses.
- Ensure that sufficient time has been set aside for the mediation and bear in mind that in order for the mediation session to work effectively, the parties may need time to vent their feelings and consider their positions before moving forward with a resolution.
- Prepare your case thoroughly and do not underestimate the amount of preparation time that is required to get ready for the mediation, especially readying your client for the mediation.

- Prepare your client adequately for the mediation session. (See Chapter 4, "Preparing Your Client for Mediation", for a detailed description of what is required.)
- Allow your client to talk at the mediation and express his or her ideas and feelings. Do not inhibit emotional outbursts on the part of your client, but monitor them and provide the appropriate control when necessary. However, be mindful that some models of mediation may restrict such involvement.
- Avoid an adversarial approach and listen carefully to the other side's statements and their analysis of their issues and interests (unless an adversarial approach is unavoidable or deemed beneficial). Always avoid rudeness and insulting behaviour towards your opponent.
- Ensure that you allow the opponent and the opponent's lawyer to speak.
- Although being conciliatory can be helpful, avoid being overly cooperative or you may not properly serve your client's interests.
- Maintain a flexible outlook and encourage your client to also do so.
- Avoid presenting, at the outset, your "bottom line" to the mediator, even in confidence, as a settlement position should be flexible and be based on new insights and new information gained during the mediation process. (However, it should be kept in mind that at some point, you may need to advise the mediator of your bottom line position.)
- Be prepared to shift your bottom line position and be prepared for some resistance to that shift from your client.
- Do not refuse to make a counter offer to an offer that you find insulting or inappropriate.
- Demonstrate good faith efforts to settle the case but at the same time, make it clear that you and your client are ready, willing and able to try the case. If you appear overly weak, the settlement may be compromised.
- Do not attempt to slip in terms after the fact that have not been agreed to. Be thorough in developing your settlement documents.

11. THE "DO'S" OF MEDIATION

Just as there are many pitfalls that are to be avoided at all costs, there are a vast number of things that a lawyer should keep in mind at a mediation session to ensure that his or her client's interests are properly represented. The following is a list of some of those key points:

- Do not be reluctant to talk to the mediator about what you need from him or her in terms of style and needs and do not hesitate to share special characteristics of your client where appropriate.
- Be prepared to encourage your client to concede points that are of little importance to your client.
- Show an understanding of the opponent's position and show compassion when appropriate and genuine.
- Be patient with your client, your opponent and the mediator.
- Avoid causing the worsening of the relationship between your client and his or her opponent.

12. ETHICAL AND PROFESSIONAL ISSUES

There are a number of ethical and professional issues that you as employment counsel may face in the context of mediation. Although most counsel will be clear on their ethical and professional obligations with respect to general practice issues as well as issues that arise in the litigation process, there may be some ambiguity with respect to what the obligations of counsel are in the conduct of a mediation. At mediation, unlike examinations for discovery and trial, no evidence is given by witnesses under oath. Clearly, in a legal proceeding, where you are aware that your client is lying or is doing something you consider to be dishonest or dishonourable, you must not knowingly assist or permit your client to do so. For instance, you may not allow a client to testify if you know that he or she is going to lie on the witness stand.[3]

Arguably, this age-old principle would apply to mediation proceedings, despite the fact that no evidence is given under oath. For instance, suppose the opposing counsel or mediator asks your client what his or her employment status is in a dispute of wrongful dismissal against your client's former employer. If your client has found new employment, but deliberately misstates this fact at the mediation in hopes of achieving a higher settlement, what are your ethical obligations? On the one hand, you cannot permit your client to lie, but on the other hand, how can you extract yourself from the matter without prejudicing your client's case? The rules are clear that you may properly and ethically withdraw yourself from a file where you have good cause to do so. Furthermore, the *Rules of*

---

[3] Law Society of Upper Canada, *Rules of Professional Conduct*, effective November 1, 2000, rule 4.01(2)(b).

Professional Conduct permits you to remove yourself where your client is guilty of dishonourable conduct or where you have been deceived by your client.[4] You cannot ignore your ethical obligations and arguably, you must convince your client to correct the misstatement or conclude the mediation and possibly withdraw from the case. Depending on the circumstances, this obligation may be either mandatory or optional. If in doubt, you may wish to seek advice from the Practice Advisory of your local Law Society.

Although each case will depend on the particular circumstances of the case, practically speaking, your first step may be to pull your client aside and advise him or her that you cannot permit such dishonest conduct. You should urge your client to correct the misstatement and advise him or her of the consequences of not doing so. In preparation for the mediation, it is always prudent practice to caution your client that even though evidence is not given under oath, there is an obligation to present the facts and evidence in an honest and forthright manner. If you have particular concern that your client may engage in questionable conduct, you may warn your client of this obligation in stronger terms and advise your client that if anything is deliberately misstated to his or her personal gain, you will be required to remove yourself from the file.

Ethical considerations may also arise where a client (usually the employer in an employment law matter), wishes to use the mediation process as a tactic to intimidate the other party or to cause them to incur unnecessary legal costs and has no genuine interest in resolving the dispute. If you are aware that your client's intentions are improper, there may be ethical obligations upon you to discourage or dissuade your client from proceeding in this manner.[5] If you are counsel on the other side of a matter and it becomes clear to you that the opponent is using the mediation process as a tactic, prudent practice would dictate that you should protect your client's interest by either discontinuing the mediation session immediately or turning the tables on the other side by taking an equally aggressive stance.

What if you become aware that the opposing counsel or mediator has made a glaring mistake in the calculation of the monetary offer which is greatly beneficial to your client? Because the mediation process is often very intense and numerous offers may be fielded back and forth between the parties, there is an obvious potential for errors to be made. For instance, the mathematical calculation of salary or benefits or the length

---

[4]   *Ibid.*, rule 2.09(2), (7) and (8).
[5]   *Ibid.*, rule 2.02(5).

of notice may be inaccurate. There may be an ethical obligation upon you to advise the opposing counsel or mediator of this error when you become aware of it. The rules are clear that counsel must not take advantage of or act without fair warning upon slips, irregularities or mistakes on the part of other lawyers.[6]

Since employment law matters often involve multiple parties and since you may often represent a company as well as principals and employees of the company who are named in the action or complaint, you should be very wary of situations that lead to a conflict of interest between parties that you represent. During the course of a mediation, it may become apparent to you that the interests of one client are divergent from the interests of another. If that occurs, it may be incumbent upon you to refer the clients to other lawyers. Where the conflict becomes apparent during the course of a mediation session, it may be necessary to halt the proceedings until your clients are able to obtain independent legal advice or resolve the issue between themselves.[7]

Finally, as discussed in Chapter 2, "Determining When to Mediate", there is an express obligation on counsel in Ontario to consider the appropriateness of ADR to the resolution of issues in every case and, if appropriate, to inform the client of ADR options and, if so instructed, to take steps to pursue those options.[8] This was an interesting addition to the Ontario Rules in 1996 and signified a changing mindset within the profession to utilize ADR processes, including mediation wherever feasible. Furthermore, you have an obligation to inform your client of these options.[9] This is consistent with counsel's further obligation to advise and encourage a client to compromise or settle a dispute whenever it is possible to do so on a reasonable basis and to discourage a client from commencing useless proceedings.[10] Accordingly, you should consider the applicability and usefulness of mediation or other ADR techniques in each file and where appropriate, canvass these possibilities with your client. In Ontario, mandatory mediations have made that determination very straightforward.

There may be many other circumstances that lead to ethical dilemmas in the context of mediation. You should treat mediation as you would any other step in the legal process and at all times, be mindful of your ethical and professional obligations.

---

[6]   *Ibid.*, rule 6.03(3).
[7]   *Ibid.*, rule 2.04(9).
[8]   *Ibid.*, rule 2.02(3).
[9]   *Ibid.*, rule 2.02(3).
[10]   *Ibid.*, rule 2.02(2).

APPENDIX 5A

FORM 24.1C

(General heading)
STATEMENT OF ISSUES

(To be provided to mediator and parties at least seven days before the mediation session)

1. Factual and legal issues in dispute

The plaintiff (*or* defendant) states that the following factual and legal issues are in dispute and remain to be resolved.

(Issues should be stated briefly and numbered consecutively.)

2. Party's position and interests (what the party hopes to achieve)

(Brief summary.)

3. Attached documents

Attached to this form are the following documents that the plaintiff (*or* defendant) considers of central importance in the action: *(list)*

(date)   *(party's signature)*
                                     (Name, address, telephone number and fax
                                     number of lawyer of party filing statement of
                                     issues, or of party)

NOTE: When the plaintiff provides a copy of this form to the mediator, a copy of the pleadings shall also be included.

NOTE: Rule 24.1.14 provides as follows:

All communications at a mediation session and the mediator's notes and records shall be deemed to be without prejudice settlement discussions.

APPENDIX 5B

FORM 24.1C — EXAMPLE

Court File No._____

SUPERIOR COURT OF JUSTICE

BETWEEN:

JOHN SMITH

Plaintiff

- and -

ABC TRUST CO.

Defendant

STATEMENT OF ISSUES

1. Factual and Legal Issues in Dispute

The defendant states that the following factual and legal issues are in dispute and remain to be resolved.

1. Whether there was just cause for the termination of the plaintiff's employment?
2. If there is no just cause, what is the period of reasonable notice?
3. Has the plaintiff taken adequate steps to mitigate damages?
4. Is the plaintiff entitled to damages for the intentional infliction of mental distress, aggravated or punitive damages?

2. Party's Position and Interests (what the party hopes to achieve)

The plaintiff was employed with the defendant for a period of approximately 8 years, most recently in the position of Client Service

Representative. The plaintiff was responsible for processing financial transactions, including mutual funds transactions on behalf of the defendant's clients. In this role, the plaintiff was required to comply with established policies and procedures. In addition, as a registered mutual fund representative, the plaintiff was required to sign an acknowledgment on an annual basis indicating that he had read and understood the policies and procedures and would comply with them on an ongoing basis.

The plaintiff breached the established policies and procedures of the defendant on a number of occasions. The plaintiff was repeatedly advised of his performance deficiencies, both verbally and in writing. Despite verbal warnings throughout 2012, the plaintiff's performance failed to improve and he was provided with written notice on October 11, 2012. The plaintiff had made serious errors in breach of the defendant's policies and procedures which resulted in financial losses to the defendant. This warning letter was provided to the plaintiff following a meeting which took place with his manager.

The letter of October 11, 2012, sets out the following serious errors:

(1) The plaintiff conducted mutual fund transactions on several occasions without obtaining proper written instructions from the client, in breach of Mutual Fund Compliance. The plaintiff alleges that it was common practice and knowledge that written instructions were not required on transactions which were less than $1,000. The defendant denies that there is any such exemption. In any event, all of the transactions in question were in excess of $1,000.

(2) The plaintiff processed a transaction without ensuring that a proper Power of Attorney had been obtained from the client.

The plaintiff raised no objections to the written warning of October 11, 2012, and signed the letter.

The plaintiff was provided with a second letter of warning dated November 10, 2012, as he had committed a further serious error by knowingly processing a transaction on or about November 7, 2012, without the client's consent. The client personally came to the branch to express his dissatisfaction and lack of consent to the terms of the transaction.

The plaintiff was clearly advised that failure to improve his performance would result in the termination of his employment with just cause. Despite this, the defendant became aware of a further serious breach on the part of the plaintiff which amounted to wilful misconduct. These actions were deliberate and intentional and executed by the plaintiff with the clear intention of misleading the defendant.

The plaintiff processed a transaction on or about November 22, 2012, on the instructions of the sister of a client of the defendant. The plaintiff falsely advised the defendant that he had obtained a Power of Attorney from the client the previous year and assured the defendant that the transaction was therefore appropriate. Following that, the plaintiff proceeded to obtain a Power of Attorney on or about December 6, 2012, and inserted the date of November 10, 2012, a date which pre-dated the date of the original transaction, that being November 22, 2012. On or about December 7, 2012, the plaintiff admitted that he entered the date on the Power of Attorney with the intention of ensuring that the date was prior to the date of the original transaction. This action on the part of the plaintiff amounts to just cause for termination.

In any event, the wilful misconduct coupled with the continuous serious performance deficiencies over an extended period of time clearly amount to just cause for termination. The plaintiff clearly understood what changes in his performance were required. Despite this, the plaintiff refused all offers of one-on-one coaching and administration time.

The defendant's level of scrutiny and supervision of the plaintiff's work were appropriate in view of the deteriorating quality of work performed by the plaintiff. The defendant denies that it subjected the plaintiff to a humiliating, distressing or deliberate course of action and the plaintiff's conduct was investigated in the same manner as would be any other employee in similar circumstances. The defendant denies that the plaintiff has suffered mental distress and further, states that if he has suffered mental distress it was not the result of any inappropriate or high handed conduct on the part of the defendant.

The defendant denies that the plaintiff is entitled to any damages.

There has been little or no negotiation in respect of this matter, in view of the clearly divergent views of the parties.

3. Attached Documents

Attached to this form are the following documents that the defendant considers of central importance in the action:

1. Letter of warning dated October 11, 2012, and signed Acknowledgment by John Smith.
2. Letter of warning dated November 10, 2012, and signed Acknowledgment by John Smith.
3. Mutual Fund Guidelines for Salesperson Acknowledgment dated July 7, 2012, signed by John Smith.
4. General Power of Attorney re Brian White dated November 10, 2012.
5. Letter of termination dated December 7, 2012.

Date:_____

_____
Party's Signature
Solicitors for the Defendant

NOTE: When the plaintiff provides a copy of this form to the mediator, a copy of the pleadings shall also be included.

NOTE: Rule 24.1.14 provides as follows:

All communications at a mediation session and the mediator's notes and records shall be deemed to be without prejudice settlement discussions.

Chapter 6

THE MEDIATION PROCESS

Although there are many stages that are common to all mediation sessions, there is not unanimous agreement as to the number of stages in a typical mediation session. Many of the stages of mediation overlap and are intertwined and it is sometimes difficult to separate them into distinct stages. Due to the unique characteristics of the parties and the distinct nature of each dispute, no two employment mediation sessions will proceed in exactly the same manner even where the same mediator presides over both mediation sessions. This is because mediation is a fluid and flexible process that is largely controlled by the parties themselves.

Mediators typically divide a mediation into as few as four stages and as many as twelve stages. These differences depend on the methods of categorization used as well as whether the preparatory stages are included within these categories. Regardless of the number of stages, during a typical mediation session, the parties will generally progress from problem-defining stages to problem-solving stages. Within this broad spectrum, the stages are quite flexible in order to accommodate the individual needs and interests of each party. We have divided the mediation process into seven distinct stages that seem to best suit the vast majority of employment mediations. There are other distinct mediation processes that do not closely follow these stages, which will be discussed later in this chapter. The stages are identified as follows:

- Pre-session preparation
- Introduction
- Information exchange, defining the issues and generating an agenda
- Issue exploration
- Generating settlement options and problem solving
- Development of final agreement
- Closing session

The first three stages in this categorization are classified as "problem-defining" and the final four stages are classified as "problem-solving". Experience dictates that where more time is spent in the "problem-defining" phase, there is less likelihood of substantial impasses and greater likelihood that the parties will achieve an acceptable resolution. This chapter will describe in detail the typical mediation process used in employment mediations. There is obviously considerable variance from one mediation to another. At the end of the chapter, we will highlight other distinct mediation processes.

1. PRE-SESSION PREPARATION

Pre-session preparation includes all of the events that take place prior to the date of the scheduled mediation session. These have been addressed in detail in Chapters 2 through 5. This includes selecting the mediator and communicating with the mediator prior to the mediation session. Typically, the mediation agreement will be reviewed and signed by each party prior to their attendance at the mediation. Pre-session preparation also includes the preparation of the parties' respective cases and the submission and exchange of pre-mediation materials.

2. INTRODUCTION

It is incumbent upon the mediator to establish a comfortable and cooperative atmosphere at the outset of the mediation session. Proper introductions are important in order to set a positive tone and put the parties at ease with the mediator (and with each other, where possible). The mediator normally commences the session by introducing himself or herself to the parties and counsel. The mediator may also direct the parties on the seating arrangements. In some cases, the parties and/or counsel may not have met one another previously, and if so, the mediator will oversee these introductions. The mediator may ask for the exchange of business cards and ascertain what names or titles will be used during the mediation session. In most employment law mediations, the parties will already be acquainted by virtue of their employment relationship. Therefore, in most employment mediations, the use of first names is preferable and it will also help to set a more informal and relaxed tone for the mediation session. Most mediators will also want to be addressed by their first names.

There may be other matters that should be dealt with at this preliminary stage such as addressing time restrictions that may exist for the parties, their counsel or the mediator. It is important to be upfront about such time restrictions so that the mediator can properly structure and pace the mediation process. It will also prevent one party from being surprised at a sudden interruption by the opponent which may disrupt the progress made towards a resolution. The mediator may also wish to place certain restrictions on the use of cellular telephones and other devices in order to avoid unnecessary disruptions.

The introduction stage will likely only last a few minutes but it serves the important purpose of "breaking the ice" and establishing a comfortable rapport between the parties and the mediator as well as between the parties themselves. A good mediator will be able to assess the comfort levels of the parties at this stage and adapt his or her style accordingly to ensure the greatest ease of communication. Certainly, good communication between the parties and with the mediator increases the odds of settlement.

In the next step of the introduction phase, the mediator will define his or her role in the mediation process as an impartial third party who is entrusted with the task of facilitating the process. The mediator may also describe his or her credentials and experience in mediating employment law disputes. The mediator will also explain in very simple terms the nature and objectives of the mediation process, although presumably, if they are sufficiently prepared, the parties will be aware of this. The mediator will wish to establish an optimistic tone and may refer to his or her strong commitment to the mediation process, the success rate of employment law mediations as well as the benefits to the parties of reaching an amicable resolution. The mediator may commend the parties for agreeing to attempt to mediate a resolution to their dispute.

At this stage, the mediator will also wish to verify that the parties have the authority to settle the case. If not, the mediator will ensure that arrangements have been made to obtain proper and necessary instructions during the course of the mediation session. If it is determined at some point that one or both parties will not be able to obtain instructions, the mediation session may be adjourned. Alternatively, arrangements may be made to allow a representative to be involved through means such as Skype.

In his or her introductory statement, the mediator will also likely set some basic ground rules for the conduct of the proceedings which may include a requirement that the parties not interrupt one another and that they demonstrate mutual courtesy and respect. Where the mediation is voluntary, the mediator will also inform the parties of their right to terminate the session at any stage and for any reason. As previously stated, this right may not exist in mandatory mediations. The mediator will also describe the likely order of the proceedings but will emphasize that this is subject to change at any time depending on the course of events.

The mediator will also likely confirm at this stage that the parties understand that the discussions will be confidential and that all settlement positions will be conveyed on a without prejudice basis.

Before proceeding to the next stage, the mediator should summarize in very general terms his or her understanding of what the parties wish to accomplish at the mediation session. In addition, the mediator should address any questions the parties may have about the mediation process.

3. INFORMATION EXCHANGE, DEFINING THE ISSUES AND GENERATING AN AGENDA

At the commencement of the next stage of the mediation session, each party will typically be given an opportunity to present an opening statement. As mentioned previously, this stage is often opted out of based on time constraints. The utility of this step needs to be considered in each case. If opening statements are presented, counsel and/or the parties will present their version of the facts and issues they hope to resolve. To make the most effective use of the mediation process, the parties should be encouraged to define their issues as interests rather than as positions or legal rights.

Normally, the plaintiff or complainant (which in most employment mediations is the employee) will present his or her case first. However, where the mediation involves a "for cause" termination, the mediator may wish the employer to present its case first as the onus of proof in a cause termination would rest with the company. Where the mediation involves difficult or sensitive issues of discrimination or sexual harassment, the mediator may allow the complainant to present his or her case last in order to allow the complainant to attain a certain level of comfort with the mediation process. The speaker is normally allowed an opportunity to provide his or her oral presentation in an uninterrupted manner and no questions are generally asked until the presentation is complete. At this time, the mediator may ask open-ended questions or an occasional clarifying question but he or she will not generally ask detailed, sensitive or intrusive questions. These sorts of questions may be reserved for the private sessions. Usually, questions are directed through the mediator and are not directed from one party or his or her counsel to the other. It is important for all participants to remember that this is not a discovery process.

Each party will be given approximately the same length of time to present his or her case. However, the overall length of time allocated to this stage will obviously depend on the complexity of the case and the number of issues, as well as the particular characteristics of the parties including their apparent level of comfort with the process. Where the mediation evokes emotional responses for one or both parties, or the issues are particularly personal or sensitive in nature, the opening remarks may be prolonged. It will need to be assessed how beneficial it is to allow significant time for this stage. Of course, it partly depends on the amount of time allotted for the mediation session.

Based on the information presented in each party's opening statement as well as in the written mediation materials, the mediator will quickly endeavour to identify existing areas of agreement between the parties. For example, at the very least, there may be a broad area of agreement such as the desire to salvage the employment relationship in an internal "workplace mediation". In situations where the employment relationship has ended, the parties may agree on certain aspects of the individual's performance or compensation terms. Commonly, the mediator will seek an agreement between the parties with respect to the value of an employee's compensation on a monthly and on an annual basis. That way, if a resolution involves payment of severance, all parties will be in agreement as to the calculation used. It also lessens the margin of error when the parties are presenting offers back and forth during the mediation session. Of course, at times, the amount of monthly/annual compensation will be in dispute which will not allow this determination to be made at the outset of the mediation session. Where the dispute involves allegations of harassment or discrimination, the parties may agree on certain facts, but disagree on their context or on the legal ramifications of such factual findings. Where employment has ended, the parties will also likely agree that a common goal is for the employee to re-employ. The parties may also agree on certain procedural aspects such as the desire to avoid litigation as well as the undue expense and delays associated with litigation. By identifying these common areas, no matter how general, the parties will be reminded that there is some common ground between them which may make the task of settling the case appear less onerous. Sometimes parties cannot see these commonalities without the assistance of a neutral mediator. By bringing this to their attention, the mediator will also establish an optimistic tone for the negotiations. The parties may suddenly be under the impression that their views are not as divergent as they initially thought they were before they entered the mediation room.

The mediator may then assist the parties in setting an agenda for the balance of the mediation session. In consultation with the parties, the mediator will develop a list of issues that are in dispute and require resolution. The mediator will attempt to define these issues in terms that are as neutral as possible in an effort to avoid isolating either party. These issues will also be prioritized in the order in which they will be further discussed. It often assists the parties to list the issues in priority order with visual aids such as a flip chart or smart board. When the parties can actually see the issues in written form and can strike each issue off the list as each gets resolved, it may provide some encouragement to the parties that a resolution may be possible as well as a sense that progress is being made.

Through this exercise, the parties, with the assistance of the mediator, will be able to discern their dispute with greater clarity and understanding. In addition, the parties will likely be able to more clearly identify the most important interests of their opponent, which may be different from what they had themselves defined as the opponent's interests during their pre-mediation preparation.

Often, the mediator will summarize the verbal presentation of each party in order to verify the accuracy of what was presented and to demonstrate to the parties his or her understanding of the case as presented. It also reinforces each party's position and ensures that the other party understands what that position is.

4. ISSUE EXPLORATION

Once the parties enter the issue exploration stage, they will have progressed to the "problem-solving" mode of the mediation session. If sufficient time is spent in the preparatory stage, the task at hand should now appear very clear to the parties. A substantial amount of time is normally spent in the issue-exploration stage. The purpose of this stage is to involve the parties in a process of constructive negotiation. It is at this stage that the process may become very creative and will be flexible and fluid in order to meet the needs and interests of the parties.

It will be the mediator's responsibility to facilitate the discussions at this stage, by utilizing a variety of skills and styles. The mediator will provide a sense of order to this phase by ensuring that the parties progress through their agenda and focus on one agenda item at a time. The manner in which the mediator conducts this phase will depend on the type of mediation method used. For instance, in a facilitative mediation, the mediator may use strategies to encourage the parties and their counsel to communicate directly with one another. The parties may ask questions of one another about matters that were raised in the opening statement and which require clarification. The mediator will refrain from intervening except where it will assist the parties in the communication process. At this stage, the parties are often encouraged to openly communicate with one another, rather than through the mediator.

If the mediation proceeds as an evaluative or settlement mediation, the mediator will play a more active role at this stage and may direct all communication through himself or herself by asking questions of the parties and possibly suggesting options.

While exploring issues, the parties may exchange their perceptions of events that have occurred. In other words, each party will state the facts as he or she sees them. This may assist in "clearing the air" between the parties which may allow them to focus their attention on the real issues at hand. This can be a therapeutic exercise for the parties, particularly for an employee in an employment law dispute. It may allow the employee to explain his or her motivations for past conduct, the significance of events as well as his or her feelings and emotions surrounding the events. For instance, an employee may express his or her views as to why he or she deems the employer's conduct as unfair, how it could have been handled differently and how it has impacted the employee. This can assist the employer in truly understanding the employee's feelings and humanizing the situation. On the flip side, the employer may sincerely state that no harm was intended, that they are sorry for any distress that was caused and/or demonstrate that there were legitimate business reasons for the employer's actions. This may lead to a greater understanding of the conduct and ultimately, an acceptance of such conduct on the employee's part.

5. GENERATING SETTLEMENT OPTIONS AND PROBLEM SOLVING

As the parties enter this stage, they may be encouraged by the mediator to suggest options for resolution, regardless of their opponent's reaction. The parties may participate in brainstorming sessions that will generate a list of potential and creative settlement options. Practice dictates that joint brainstorming will lead to a wider array of settlement options than separately generating options. In some employment mediations, the parties may be overly emotional or uncomfortable if required to work together to generate these options. In fact, joint brainstorming is probably rarely used in employment law mediations but could be more readily utilized, where the case permits it. In addition, they may perceive an unequal bargaining power. It will be up to the mediator and the parties to determine the most suitable approach while taking into account the particular circumstances of the case. The parties will also be encouraged to maintain an open mind and think in creative terms.

The theory underlying mediation is that once the mediator has assisted the parties in moving through their individual perspectives and has encouraged them to understand the dispute from the opposing party's point of view, the parties are more likely to come up with solutions that will effectively serve both of their interests. Normally, a broad range of options will be considered before they are narrowed to specific agreements. The parties will be encouraged to evaluate the options in terms of their mutual needs and interests and to select those that will satisfy the interests of both parties. The parties should engage in a process of reality testing which will help them explore the advantages, disadvantages, implications and feasibility of each option. The parties will be encouraged to consider agreements "in principle" and then proceed to fine-tune the issues by considering matters of detail. In evaluating and selecting these options, the parties may require external advice on a number of points including advice on legal, financial and taxation issues. The structure of a settlement payment can often have a great impact on the saleability of an option to a particular party. As will be outlined in the next chapter, there often is some flexibility permitted in employment law matters in terms of the structure of a settlement.

It is sometimes necessary for the parties to bargain with one another by trading off certain points against others. The parties may either make concessions or agree to split the difference in order to close the gap between them.

At any point during this process, the parties may break off into separate rooms which are often referred to as "caucuses" or "break out" sessions. If the joint session is proceeding well, it may not be necessary to break into caucuses. However, in most employment mediations, some caucusing will occur as the parties are often not at ease discussing all points on a joint basis. Usually, the financial aspects of an offer are discussed in caucus sessions. During a caucus session, each party is given an opportunity to refer to concerns or issues that they are unable to address in the joint meetings. These sessions also allow the mediators an opportunity to seek additional information in private and to better understand each party's motivations and objectives. The mediator may also be able to decipher obstacles that may be hindering productive negotiations. An important feature of the caucus is that it allows the mediator to test the feasibility of the various proposed settlement options for each party. Where parties are quite far apart in their expectations, the mediator may separately assist the parties into taking a hard look at the weaknesses in their respective cases. The mediator may even apply some pressure to each of the parties, which would not be possible in the joint sessions without looking like the mediator was favouring one side over another.

Separate sessions can take place any number of times and at any stage(s) of the mediation. In cases where parties are uncomfortable with the mediation process or they are reluctant to sit face-to-face with their opponent, they may be separated immediately at the outset of the mediation. The mediator must be astute at recognizing those circumstances where separating the parties is necessary. In a dispute involving sensitive issues of discrimination or sexual harassment, this may often be necessary. There may even be rare circumstances where the parties never meet in a joint session because emotions are running too high. This would be most common in a sexual harassment dispute and not surprisingly, it is common practice in mediation sessions conducted by the Ontario Human Rights Tribunal. It may also occur in those cases where there is a high level of acrimony, as will be discussed later in this chapter. It is also common to separate into caucuses when there appears to be a breakdown in the negotiations or the parties have become deadlocked or uncooperative. There may be other cases where the parties are unwilling or unable to provide feasible settlement options in their opponent's presence. Although often initiated by the mediator, the parties or their counsel may request a caucus session. Some would argue that such caucus sessions should be used infrequently as separating the parties may serve to reinforce the detachment and division that exists between the parties and may detract from any progress that has been achieved between the parties. However, they are used frequently and often add to the effectiveness of a mediation and increase the chance of reaching a resolution in a quick and efficient manner.

There may be other potential problems with the use of caucus sessions. Without suggesting that there is anything at all nefarious on the part of the mediator, some parties may become distrustful if the mediator meets with their opponent in private. For some individual parties, it may engender suspicion that the mediator is favouring the company's side. It is not uncommon for an employee in an employment mediation to feel such suspicion or mistrust, especially when they are already feeling wronged by the actions of the employer which led to the dispute. Often, the mediator will choose to spend a bit more time with the employee and his or her counsel to avoid this potential appearance of favouritism which the employee will likely be most sensitive to. By meeting privately, it may also appear to the parties that the mediator is exerting greater control over the process than they had expected. There may also be concern on the part of the parties that the mediator will inadvertently disclose information to one party that was shared by the other party in confidence. As the mediator will be digesting a considerable amount of information in a short period of time, it is not difficult to see how such problems could arise. It is also possible that by holding caucus sessions, the mediator may exert some influence over the result by transmitting offers back and forth from one party to the other. This is because the mediator will have some latitude with respect to how the offer is packaged and presented from one party to the other. This may in fact deprive the parties, to a certain extent, of their decision-making responsibilities. By shuttling back and forth between the parties, there is also a risk that the mediator will inadvertently miscommunicate information. Notwithstanding these concerns, holding caucus sessions can be useful and in many cases, these sessions may be the key to reaching a satisfactory resolution.

Normally, once the caucuses have taken place and their purpose has been served, the parties will reconvene in a joint session.

6. AGREEMENT AND CLOSING SESSION

Irrespective of whether the parties are able to reach an agreement, the mediation session should end on a positive note. Unfortunately, that is not always the case as you will see in the next section. If the parties had been separated into caucuses, they should most times be reconvened prior to concluding the mediation session. Where the parties have reached an agreement, or are close to concluding an agreement, they may engage in further joint discussions and may work together to resolve the finer details of the settlement in a final joint session. The mediator should ensure that all issues have been dealt with and that no points of interest to one or both parties have been overlooked. Where the relationship is fairly amicable, it is often a good measure for the parties to convene while counsel fine-tunes the settlement documents together. This would be even more imperative where the parties will be continuing an employment relationship.

Even where it has become apparent that a resolution cannot be reached, the parties may reconvene so that the mediator can highlight those issues that have been resolved or narrowed between the parties. The hope is that the parties will leave the session feeling that the mediation was productive. The parties may discuss what steps they will take next to pursue their interests. For instance, they may discuss whether a further mediation would be worthwhile. At times, impasses will occur in an employment mediation because the parties are lacking important information such as medical documentation, compensation information or performance documentation. In a case of sexual harassment or other complaint, it may be determined that the investigation that was conducted was incomplete and that further investigation must take place or further witnesses should be interviewed. Perhaps it was determined that a key company representative needs to be involved in order to maximize the chances of resolution. If so, the parties may agree to reconvene at a future date once the necessary information has been obtained or the necessary steps have been completed. Alternatively, other forms of dispute resolution such as arbitration or mediation/arbitration may be suggested. The parties may also agree that a resolution is not possible and that moving to the next phase of litigation is the best course of action.

If the parties have successfully reached a resolution, the settlement should be carefully documented and executed through written minutes of settlement. The terms of the agreement and the key elements of the settlement should be outlined. Where counsel has attended the mediation with clients, counsel for one party may take the initiative of drawing up the agreement with the input of the other counsel. Where counsel has not attended the mediation, the parties themselves may draft the agreement or the mediator may be called upon to do so, although this is not preferable. In fact, this situation is potentially problematic because the mediator will be at risk of taking on an advisory role that he or she should definitely be avoiding. Having said that, at a mediation at the Ontario Human Rights Tribunal, the mediators typically draft the agreement but it is largely because the agreement needs to comply with the tribunal's requirements. In these cases, the mediator will encourage the parties to review the terms of the proposed settlement with their independent counsel prior to execution. Where the parties choose not to avail themselves of the right to counsel, the agreement should confirm that the parties are aware of their right to independent legal advice. Where the terms are somewhat complex, they may be concisely identified in writing at the mediation session and referred back to counsel to draft the agreement in proper legal terms. Although it is normally preferable to execute the agreement at the mediation session when there is both momentum and a meeting of the minds, this may not always be feasible, especially where an unrepresented party wishes to involve counsel in the terms of settlement. Even so, an agreement could be outlined that could be made subject to each party obtaining independent legal advice. Sometimes even where counsel is present at the mediation, brief minutes of settlement will be drafted and signed. Following the mediation session, counsel will draft more comprehensive minutes of settlement that elaborate on the basic terms of settlement. A cautionary note however — this can sometimes lead to negotiation after a deal has been reached so closure of the matter remains "up in the air" and the settlement may fail.

The agreement should clearly state what each party is expected to do and should include specific dates for the completion of these terms. Dates provide certainty. Dates are also important so that expectations are set and so that litigation can ensue if any term is breached. Even where counsel is present to draft the agreement, the parties may wish to seek independent advice from other professionals, in particular financial, medical or taxation advice. If so, the parties may agree to the terms in principle, subject to a party's right to obtain the necessary advice.

Whether or not a resolution has been reached, the mediator will want to close the mediation session on a positive note and make some closing remarks, commending the parties on their efforts.

7. POST-MEDIATION ACTIVITIES

Even where the parties have brought their proper representatives to the mediation, at times, the resolution reached may require ratification by external bodies such as boards and councils. This may be especially applicable for non-profit charitable organizations and public sector organizations. If ratification is necessary, the terms of settlement will be entered on the basis that the settlement is conditional on obtaining this approval. In many cases, this will merely be a "rubber stamp" but nonetheless, a necessary formality to ensure the legality of the agreement reached. Sometimes, settlement may even require the approval of an unrelated body. For instance, if one of the terms of settlement of an employment law dispute relates to an award of stock options or share purchase, the approval of a governing body such as the Toronto Stock Exchange or the Ontario Securities Commission may be required. In many wrongful dismissal settlements, where the employee has collected employment insurance benefits, it may be necessary to obtain a statement from Human Resources Development Canada with respect to the employee's employment insurance repayment obligations, which amount will be required to be paid out of the settlement funds.

In other employment law cases, the ratification by a court or external authority such as the applicable Human Rights Tribunal or Workplace Safety and Insurance Board may be required. The relevant employment tribunal may need to ensure that the proposed settlement is consistent with the tribunal's jurisdiction and relevant policy requirements.[1]

8. MEDIATION PROCESS IN A "WORKPLACE MEDIATION"

Many of the steps addressed above will also apply to the conduct of an internal "workplace mediation". However, there are some special steps and circumstances that should be considered in the context of a workplace mediation. Typically, the parties will be unrepresented by counsel. The following steps are often followed by the mediator when setting up a workplace mediation:

1. The mediator will contact each party to the dispute and may meet with each party individually in advance of the mediation session.
2. The mediator will listen to each party's story, needs, concerns and fears about the process. The mediator may listen to the party's perspective of the conflict and request specific examples of the behaviour in question. The mediator will also want to hear what the party has done to address the conflict and what his or her hopes and goals are from the process.
3. The mediator will explain the mediation process to each party. The mediator will advise each party of the ground rules for the mediation session. This includes treating other parties with respect and honesty and listening to others during the session. The mediator will also answer questions about the process. The meeting with each party will normally be conducted by the mediator off-site from the employer's premises.
4. The mediator will also explain the confidentiality of the process as well as the voluntary nature of the mediation, meaning that either party may walk away from the mediation process at any time.
5. The mediator will also advise that although the goal of the mediation session is to resolve the conflict, the agreement is not

---

[1] See Chapter 8, "Special Issues in Mediating Employment Law Disputes", which discusses mediations involving the Human Rights Tribunal.

necessarily a legally binding agreement. This means that a party still has the right to file a formal complaint or lawsuit if the resolution proves not to be satisfactory to them. This is a distinct difference from a resolution reached through mediation of an employment litigation matter. In those matters, the agreement is always intended to be legally binding.

6. Each party will be asked to sign an agreement to mediate prior to the start of the session.

It is normally most effective if the workplace mediation takes place as quickly as possible. There is a better chance of resolution where the dispute has just arisen and before the parties become overly entrenched in their positions. Typically, early on in the conflict, before the matter has festered, there will be more resolution options available to the parties than might be available later on.

The mediation should take place off-site from the employer's premises wherever possible. The conduct of the mediation session during a workplace mediation may not differ much from the conduct of a post-employment mediation where the parties are embroiled in litigation. However, there is a much higher likelihood that the parties will be unrepresented by counsel. Parties may request that they bring along a trusted adviser such as a close friend or family member and this is often allowed as long as the adviser also agrees to be bound by the duty of confidentiality. Since the parties are likely to be unrepresented, the mediator must take extra precautions to ensure that he or she remains neutral and is perceived by the parties as remaining neutral. Like any other mediation, the mediator's role will be to facilitate communication between the parties and assist the parties in clarifying their needs as well as understanding each other's positions. The mediator may play an active role in exploring settlement options. The mediator should focus on the agenda of the mediation session and keep the process on track. The mediator should ensure that the parties are listening to one another, remaining respectful of one another and following the guidelines.

At the outset of the workplace mediation session, the parties will likely convene in a joint session followed by separate sessions where the parties can each participate in issue exploration. In many workplace mediations, the parties may at all times work together in a joint session exploring issues and resolution. A shuttle mediation process may not be necessary depending on the needs of the parties and the issues being addressed.

THE MEDIATION PROCESS

The model of mediation that often is most effective for use during a workplace mediation is the transformative model. The nature of a transformative mediation allows the parties to discuss what each person thinks is important and what they would like their opponent to understand about their case. Through the transformative mediation process, the parties can gain enhanced self-empowerment and allow them to "transform" the quality of their interaction. The result of this process is that they have clarified the underlying conflict and have allowed for acceptable and lasting outcomes. In a transformative mediation, each party holds a veto power to withdraw from the mediation. If at any time during the process, a party starts to feel uncomfortable, the party can ask to speak privately with the mediator and decide how they can address their discomfort with the other side.

The workplace mediation process can provide the parties with very useful insight into their own behaviour. It may cause the parties to reflect on their own behaviour and what role they may have played in the conflict. It allows the parties to use the energy generated by the conflict in a positive manner.

Although a face to face mediation with all parties present is normally the most effective process, there are times when a workplace mediation can be conducted through a video or teleconference or even through back and forth telephone calls and emails with the mediator. Skype interviews may also be a useful tool where the parties cannot convene together. Certainly, many of the benefits of the process are lost when a face to face mediation is not done, but there still may be some positive results gained from a simplified and less personal approach.

A workplace mediation will usually result in non-financial resolutions as the parties are most focused on salvaging the employment relationship. Accordingly, the parties and the mediators need to be creative in designing an effective resolution to the conflict. The focus is usually on how the parties can move forward from their conflict in a positive way. The worst outcome of a workplace mediation would be for the conflict to worsen and the mediator must work hard to ensure that the process does not cause a greater flare up of poor relations between the parties.

If an agreement is reached, the mediator will assist with drafting the memorandum of agreement. The mediator may also provide the employer with a progress report which will highlight any necessary details of the resolution, whether any additional meetings are required and anything further that the employer needs to do to facilitate communication between the parties. The details cannot normally be kept confidential from the employer as the employer will be responsible for overseeing the implementation of the agreement and ensuring that each party satisfies his or her obligations.

Regardless of whether a resolution was reached, it is good practice for the employer to follow up with each party shortly after the completion of the mediation session to assess with the parties whether the mediation session was helpful, whether any additional support is required for any party and to determine whether any follow up session is required. Where the conflict arose between two employees or an employee and manager, the employer should take steps to monitor the relationship for awhile and regularly check in with the parties to see how things are going. If the relationship worsens again, it would be important to try to take immediate steps to address the problem.

Where no agreement has been reached as a result of a workplace mediation, parties may still find that there has been an improvement in their relationship. Over time, the matter may resolve itself without any further intervention. Alternatively, a further mediation may be helpful at a later date.

9. ALTERNATIVE MEDIATION PROCESSES

(a) "Judicial" Mediation

As discussed earlier in this chapter, there are a number of variations from the "typical" employment law mediation process. One approach that goes against the traditional philosophy of mediation precludes the parties from participating directly in the mediation process. We refer to this approach as the "judicial" mediation process and it is most commonly used by very senior mediators or retired judges with a mediation practice. This approach may be useful where there are either highly acrimonious relations between the parties or very divergent views of the facts.

This approach encourages the parties to prepare very comprehensive mediation materials. These materials will be much more detailed than the materials required at a typical mediation session. The parties may commence the mediation in a joint session, but the process will be very much controlled by the mediator rather than by the parties themselves. There are no opening statements made by either counsel or the parties. From the detailed mediation materials, the mediator will outline his or her understanding of the facts and issues that are deemed important to each party. The mediator will seek confirmation from the parties that the mediator has a correct understanding of the facts and issues. The mediator will develop a comprehensive outline of the issues between the parties and will delineate each party's position. This allows for clarity of all outstanding issues.

The objective of the joint session is to ensure that each side understands the position of the opponent. Throughout this process, the mediator will be doing most of the talking and will clearly be in control of the process. The initial joint session could be as short as one hour or as long as three hours, depending on the degree of complexity of the dispute.

Following the initial joint session, the parties will separate into private caucus sessions. At this stage, the parties and counsel may become more involved in the process. During the private sessions, the mediator will work at bridging the factual and issue gaps that exist between the parties. The parties will also determine the strengths and weaknesses of their respective cases with a view to analyzing settlement prospects. The parties will be directed to consider the risks of litigation if a settlement is not reached and to this end, the mediator may provide an evaluation on the likely outcome of the case. The mediator may even make some assessments of each party's credibility and convey this to each party and his or her counsel.

This kind of judicial mediation typically comprises a full-day session. Although it stays loosely within the parameters of an interest-based mediation, it is much more evaluative than the typical mediation approach. A mediation of this format will require a mediator with an extensive employment law background as the approach is very analytical in nature. In order to be effective, the mediator must be up-to-date on the current state of the law and must be able to command the full respect of counsel and their clients.

One of the clear disadvantages of this process is that the parties do not have an opportunity to express themselves in as great detail as they may in other forms of mediation, at least not in the joint sessions. This format of mediation is not recommended in situations where the parties are unrepresented by counsel and may not be cost-effective where the nature of the dispute is quite simple as it typically requires a full-day mediation and consequently, higher mediation fees.

(b) Separate Sessions

Some mediators may hold separate sessions at the outset of the mediation prior to convening the parties in a joint session. This is for the purpose of gathering information and understanding each party's concerns. This process may be preferred where the parties are inhibited from disclosing important information at the early stages of the mediation or in the presence of their opponent. This process may also be used where the parties are extremely uncomfortable confronting each other in a face-to-face setting. In employment law, this may be a particular concern in discrimination or sexual harassment cases or other complaint pursuant to the internal complaint policy. The process may also be utilized effectively in cases where the facts are complex, as it allows the mediator to assess the relevance of information in isolation in order to determine what should be included in the agenda. One clear disadvantage of separate meetings at this early stage is that the parties may misstate the facts or circumstances without the knowledge of the other party. This may put the mediator in a difficult position of trying to weed out the extraneous and non-credible information from the "real" and reliable information.

(c) Shuttle Mediation

An extension of the separate sessions approach is a process commonly known as "shuttle mediation". In shuttle mediation, the entire mediation process is conducted through separate meetings. The parties never convene jointly at any stage of the mediation. The mediator typically moves back and forth between the parties and communicates and negotiates on each party's behalf. This process is often desirable and effective where there is significant antagonism between the parties. It is also useful in cases of discrimination or sexual harassment, where joint sessions may be very emotionally difficult for the complainant — which could lead to a counterproductive mediation session. The downside of this process is that it grants to the mediator considerable power and influence as he or she is solely responsible for packaging the respective parties' positions and offers and in turn, presenting them to the other side.

(d) No Separate Meetings

Occasionally, it is considered desirable to conduct the entire mediation session on a joint basis and in these cases, the use of separate meetings will be avoided. This may be effective where there appears to be a very workable employment relationship between the parties. The benefit of this process is that it avoids any level of mistrust and suspicion that parties sometimes experience when the mediator meets with their opponent in isolation. Everything will appear to be out in the open and this can be conducive to good continuing employment relations. You would typically see this approach in a less confrontational "workplace mediation".

(e) Hybrid Process (Med-Arb)

A further alternative approach is often referred to as a "hybrid process" or more specifically, "med-arb". A med-arb approach integrates the processes of mediation and arbitration. The parties typically attempt to mediate a resolution to the conflict with the assistance of a mediator. If the mediator is unable to assist the parties in resolving the dispute through mediation, then either the same or a different third party neutral individual will issue a binding ruling on the parties. The decision will have the same force and effect as would an arbitration decision. This process gives the parties the benefits of mediation as well as a binding decision if the parties cannot reach an agreement through mediation.

In the reverse, some med-arb processes will commence with arbitration proceedings and will allow for mediation at some point during the arbitration process.

At the time of planning for a mediation, the parties should specify in their agreement to mediate whether they would be willing to attempt arbitration if mediation proves to be unsuccessful. The parties could further agree that if that non-binding process fails, they will proceed to a binding arbitration with the same neutral third party.

This combined process is usually much faster and less expensive than a regular arbitration. This is largely because the arbitrator is more knowledgeable about the case because he or she will have already gone through the mediation process with the parties. However, this process would not be appropriate where the parties want an interpretation of a contentious issue or want to set a precedent. In those cases, they would be best to proceed straight to arbitration. This process has been used in the U.S. for decades and is starting to be used more frequently in Canada. In addition to the cost benefits of combining the two processes, there may actually be a higher rate of settlement because the parties will feel the threat of an imposed settlement if they cannot reach an agreement amicably. Even if a settlement on all terms is not reached, the mediation process can serve to narrow the issues to be determined at arbitration. The one obvious downside is that the mediator/arbitrator may be privy to information from the mediation that he or she should not have in making a decision at arbitration. This process may have increasing use in employment law matters as it is fairly cost effective and combines benefits from both techniques.

The Human Rights Tribunal of Ontario has a very effective adjudication process under rule 15A.[2] When combined with the powers of the tribunal pursuant to rules 1.6 and 1.7, it creates a critical atmosphere that may allow the parties to resolve their disputes without the necessity of traditional adjudicative or adversarial procedures. The essence of the mediation adjudication agreement confirms that the party hearing the mediation can continue as the adjudicator and the parties confirm the same in a written agreement in a proscribed form. The process is generally advocated by the adjudicator at the outset of the hearing and, of course, has the critical benefit of giving each side a fairly clear understanding of what might happen during the hearing. Also, without making a decision, he or she can give the parties a good sense of the evidence that they will need to establish to be successful. That wakeup call will give the mediation adjudication a unique opportunity that is very different than any other process. The person who is doing the mediation is also the person who is doing the adjudication. That individual is obviously assessing the case, its strengths and weaknesses and being candid with the parties so that they can decide whether or not they really want to proceed to a hearing or in the alternative, find a solution that would allow for what may be a far more successful resolution. In particular, this is fundamentally important in scenarios where the employment relationship is going to continue. By combining rules 1.6 and 1.7, an adjudicator might be able, with the consent of the parties, to fashion a very short hearing on one or two critical points, thereby solving the problem in a far less costly manner, both financially and emotionally. This is certainly a unique opportunity and there is currently no specific case law in this area. The adoption of a med-arb, med-adjudication style process is perhaps the most effective way of ensuring that people get their cases heard and resolved in a setting that does not bankrupt middle class wage earners.

(f)   Co-Mediation

In some mediations, more than one mediator is used in the same mediation and this approach is commonly known as "co-mediation". Typically, co-mediation involves the use of two mediators, but sometimes three or more mediators are used. This mediation process is not commonly utilized in employment law matters but it is not uncommon

---

[2]   Human Rights Tribunal of Ontario, *Rules of Procedure*, effective July 1, 2010.

in the mediation of labour disputes where the parties are under pressure to avoid a strike situation. It is also used routinely in community and family mediations. It may be beneficial in large multi-party or complex mediations as it allows for a division of responsibilities which may increase the effectiveness of the mediation process. Typically, co-mediation comprises the same stages as does a single mediator mediation, but it may require a higher degree of preparation on the part of counsel and the mediators. The early stages may also require a differentiation of functions on the part of the mediators. For instance, during the opening statements, one mediator may engage in discussions and questioning whereas the second mediator may simply take notes. Generally, the caucus sessions will take place in the presence of both mediators rather than splitting up between the parties. This is to avoid any concerns that the mediators are taking sides and advocating one side's interests over the other. It also ensures that the mediators are provided with the same information. The application of co-mediation in employment law would be very limited given that there are typically only two parties involved with issues that typically range from uncomplicated to somewhat complicated. The co-mediation process could apply where the issues overlap with issues of patents, breach of restrictive covenants and other commercial issues that transcend normal employment law issues.

The potential advantages of co-mediation are the additional resources available with two or more mediators and the greater appearance of impartiality. In addition, co-mediation allows for the matching of each party to each mediator by age, gender, race or other characteristics of the parties, which in some cases may be the key to facilitating a resolution. This factor would have the greatest impact in discrimination and harassment cases.

There are also disadvantages to the co-mediation process. The most obvious disadvantage is the potential for increasing the costs of the process as there will be higher mediator fees and possibly a longer mediation session and greater preparation required. In addition, the matching of mediators to the attributes of the parties as outlined above may also have a downside as it could cause each party to see one mediator as an ally or supporter of his or her cause and the other as the opponent's ally. In fact, each side may select a mediator. This would be contrary to the fundamental principle of mediation that the mediators be impartial, neutral third parties.

(g) Collaborative mediation

Collaborative mediation is commonly used in the resolution of family law matters. This approach to mediation incorporates legal, emotional and financial elements in a collaborative way. It is similar to a regular mediation in that it is voluntary, non-adversarial and a form of interest-based negotiation. In a typical family mediation, the parties are not usually represented by counsel but in a collaborative process, they are both represented by separate counsel. Their counsel has special training in collaborative mediation and there is no neutral mediator present. However, the specially trained lawyers work together with their respective clients to find solutions. The collaborative model has an efficient discovery process built in whereas a straight forward mediation does not have a set information exchange process. In a collaborative approach, the parties are always in the same room and shuttle mediation is not used. Through their collective efforts, the parties (with their counsel) work together to find a resolution. This process has the potential to be expanded to employment law litigation. Provided that counsel has the proper training, a four-way resolution process can be utilized without the need for a neutral third party mediator.

APPENDIX 6A

MEDIATION PROCESS CHECKLIST

Stage 1: Pre-session preparation

- Have all of the necessary parties agreed to participate?
- Do all clients/company representatives have the requisite authority?
- Has all of the relevant information been obtained, submitted and exchanged?
- Are the ground rules of the mediation understood by all participants?
- Has a mediation agreement been signed?
- Are all necessary props, equipment and facilities available such as flip charts, computers, SMART boards and caucus rooms?

Stage 2: Introduction

- Has the mediator conducted the proper introductions?
- Have time and/or any other restrictions been identified?
- Has the mediator defined his or her role?
- Has the mediator verified that all parties have the proper authority to enter a settlement?
- Have ground rules been established, conveyed and confirmed by the mediator?

Stage 3: Information exchange, defining the issues and generating an agenda

- Presentation of opening statements and questions and answers. Is all of the necessary information available?
- If not, should the mediation be adjourned in order to obtain the necessary information?
- Have an agenda and a list of issues been developed?
- Is there a need for a caucus at this stage?

Stage 4: Issue exploration

- Have all issues been defined?

- Have the parties themselves been given the opportunity to provide their perceptions of events and express their views to either all participants or at least to the mediator?

Stage 5: Generating settlement options and problem solving

- Have options for resolution been suggested?
- Would joint brainstorming or individual brainstorming be most effective?
- Has each party evaluated the various options in terms of their own needs and interests?
- Have the options been reality tested?
- Have the parties broken off into caucus sessions if that is deemed helpful?

Stage 6: Agreement and closing session

- Have the parties been reconvened at the end of the mediation session regardless of the outcome?
- If not successful, have the parties agreed to reconvene the mediation session at a later date? If so, is further information necessary before an effective mediation can be conducted?
- If successful, have the terms of settlement been clearly documented? Has release documentation been included?
- Is approval or ratification required?
- Is independent legal or financial advice required?
- Will a more formal settlement document be prepared following the mediation?
- If litigation has ensued, and a settlement has been reached, have arrangements been made for the dismissal of the action?
- Are there time restrictions for the payment of the settlement funds?
- Are any steps from non-parties requested or required?
- Who is taking responsibility for payment of mediation fees?
- Is any tax information or documentation required?

Chapter 7

CREATIVE SOLUTIONS TO EMPLOYMENT LAW DISPUTES

1. OVERVIEW

Through mediation, parties to a dispute can open their doors to many more solutions and remedies than would be available to them if they proceeded through the traditional approach to litigation that culminates in a trial. Although employment law continues to evolve, judges are somewhat constrained in the kind of awards they are able to grant. When matters are settled outside of the courts, the parties are permitted to exercise much greater creativity in the kind of solutions they reach. Many successful settlements are achieved between parties to a dispute without the need for formal mediation. However, a mediated resolution may allow for even greater flexibility and originality in the nature of settlements, as the process itself maximizes these features. At mediation, the parties will each possess a series of trading cards that allows them to trade off one item for another, to their mutual benefit. No such trade-offs are available to the parties at a trial and often there is a clear winner and a clear loser depending on the finding of facts and the analysis of the law made by the trial judge. In this chapter, we will review the potential awards that may be granted by a court in a wrongful dismissal action and other employment related actions and we will then analyze the variations on these awards that may be achievable through mediated resolutions. We will also consider the usefulness of mediation and the creativity permitted by the resolution through mediation of non-court matters such as human rights complaints, sexual harassment complaints and internal employment disputes.

2. A COMPARISON OF SOLUTIONS: COURT AWARDS VERSUS MEDIATION

(a) Reasonable Notice

Court award

As we discussed in Chapter 1, in the absence of just cause, an employer has the right to terminate a contract of employment of indefinite duration upon the provision of reasonable notice to the terminated employee. Where the nature of the termination (cause or without cause) or the amount of reasonable notice is in dispute, these will become important points to be determined by a court. Although there is no precise formula used to calculate reasonable notice, there is clearly established case law in Canada as to what constitutes reasonable notice. Reasonable notice is based on an assessment of factors including an employee's age, length of service, position, the responsibility of the position, salary, economic circumstances of the company and marketability of the employee. The amount of reasonable notice is, therefore, fairly predictable, based on a review of similar case law. By reviewing the case law, the parties can estimate the range within which a judge will likely grant his or her award. In one decision of the Ontario Court (General Division) (now the Superior Court of Justice) a psychologist employed for a period of 24 years was awarded a notice period of 24 months.[1] In another example of the Ontario Court (General Division), a director of pharmacy who was earning $155,000 was awarded 12 months' notice based on seven years of employment with the hospital.[2] The courts will generally cap an award of reasonable notice at 24 months.

The law requires a terminated employee to take every reasonable step to obtain alternative employment during the applicable notice period. Accordingly, an award of reasonable notice by a court will be a lump sum damage payment based on the applicable months of reasonable notice less any income earned by the employee during the applicable notice period. Unless the matter proceeds to trial very quickly, the applicable notice period will typically have ceased by the date of the court's judgment and it will be a simple mathematical calculation to determine the amount of the damage award for reasonable notice. A failure to mitigate on the part of an employee may cause a judge to reduce

---

[1] *Ashman v. Orphan's Home Widows' Friend Society*, 1993 CarswellOnt 3372 (Ont. Gen. Div.).
[2] *Anderson v. Peel Memorial Hospital Assn.*, 1992 CarswellOnt 894, 40 C.C.E.L. 203, 92 C.L.L.C. 14,026 (Ont. Gen. Div.).

the award of damages that is granted. This may arise where there is evidence that an employee turned down a reasonably comparable job offer with a new employer or failed to make adequate efforts to seek new employment during the notice period.

Mediated resolution

Because mediation sessions frequently take place fairly early during the litigation process, and sometimes even prior to the commencement of litigation, the parties may reach a resolution before the applicable notice period has been completed. Accordingly, there are obvious opportunities for the parties to find a more flexible solution to the dispute than through a judgment with a mere straight damage award and a deduction for the employee's mitigation earnings. For instance, in a mediated resolution, the notice period may be payable without any regard to an employee's mitigation earnings, particularly where the mediation takes place at a very early stage in the dispute before the employee has been re-employed. In fact, an employee may be convinced to concede to a reduction in the potential notice period on the basis that it is payable by way of a lump sum payment and is not subject to any potential future mitigation earnings. Alternatively, it is common in a mediated resolution to structure the payments as a salary continuance. This typically means that the employee will be awarded with a payment equal to 50 percent of the balance of payments owing in the event the employee obtains employment prior to the end of the period of salary continuance. A court award will be a lump sum award paid retroactively. Salary continuance is not an option through a court award. A lot of employees and employers like the convenience of a salary continuance. A further variation that is possible at mediation is a resolution based on a fixed number of months (either by way of lump sum or salary continuance) with a provision for a further specified number of months to be payable in the event the employee remains unemployed at the end of the first period of notice. Alternatively, through mediation, the parties would also be at liberty to negotiate a longer period of salary continuance than would likely be awarded to the employee by a court and the parties may agree that the period of salary continuance would cease immediately upon re-employment without a 50 percent pay out or bonus to the employee. This may be of particular benefit to an employee who is very concerned about his or her likelihood of re-employment and who simply wants the reassurances and protections that come with a longer notice period. On the flip side, the employer may want regular access to a former employee's job search efforts as part of the resolution, if they have agreed to pay the employee a lengthy salary continuance.

At an early mediation, the parties can also exercise flexibility in the structure of the statutory notice and/or statutory severance payments. The parties may agree that these statutory amounts will be paid by way of salary continuance, lump sum at the beginning or end of the notice period or some combination of both.

Where a lengthy notice period is critical to an employee's interests, the employee can trade off other entitlements in order to secure this interest. One of the clear benefits of mediation is that the parties can pursue the items that are most important to them. With a court award, the parties are not able to pick and choose their remedies.

(b) Fringe Benefits

Court award

Where an employee was in receipt of fringe benefits during the course of his or her employment, a court will normally award compensation for loss of these benefits for the period of reasonable notice. For instance, if a court awards a period of reasonable notice of 12 months, the employee will also receive an award for the loss of these benefits for this period, subject to any benefits the employee received through new employment during the applicable notice period. Generally, the courts will award a pecuniary value for the lost benefits flowing from the dismissal.[3]

Mediated resolution

Benefits often become an important trading card for the parties at mediation. Some employees deem the protection of benefit coverage as critical to their interests whereas other employees are rather indifferent to the issue of compensation for lost benefits. Where unusual circumstances exist, the parties may be able to structure the benefits coverage in such a way that it is most beneficial to the employee. For instance, an employee who has a medical condition that requires expensive medications each month may be very interested in having his or her employment benefits continued, rather than receiving a fixed monthly payment in lieu of benefits (which a court would likely award). The employer may

---

[3]   *Davidson v. Allelix Inc.*, 1991 CarswellOnt 933, 7 O.R. (3d) 581, 39 C.C.E.L. 184, 86 D.L.R. (4th) 542, 54 O.A.C. 241 (Ont. C.A.).

empathize with this situation and do what they can to facilitate the continuation of benefits. Even where the parties are unable to resolve the dispute as a whole at a mediation, they may be able to reach an interim agreement on the issue of benefits which often has immediate implications to an employee. In addition, subject to the agreement of the insurer, the employer may be able to continue to insure an employee on the employer's group benefit plans for a period of time beyond a reasonable notice period. Depending on the circumstances of the case, the employer may agree to do a further extension on compassionate grounds and on the realization that this is a more cost effective way of addressing the loss of benefits. By agreeing to continue these benefits, the employer may even reduce its exposure for compensation for the loss of benefits in the event a greater notice period than it anticipated is awarded by a court. It is important to keep in mind that employers are required by employment standards legislation to continue all benefits for the duration of the statutory notice period. The continuation of benefits or compensation for the loss of benefits for the entire severance period is a common law principle. It may be less costly to the employer to continue the employee's group benefits than it would be to later compensate the employee for the loss of these benefits.

On the other hand, some employees may be willing to trade off benefits for other interests, such as an increased notice period. Benefits may be unimportant to those employees with typically low benefit usage or those employees who are able to participate in their spouses' benefit plans.

(c) Pension Losses

Court award

An employer has an obligation to compensate a terminated employee for lost pension benefits during the notice period and a court will award damages to an employee if unmade pension contributions during the notice period would have resulted in a higher pension entitlement for the employee.[4] Furthermore, if an employee's termination date is relevant for calculating the commuted value of a pension, the employer will be held liable for the difference in the pension benefit the employee would have been entitled to had the employee been permitted to work until the end of the notice period.[5] These assessments often require

---

[4]   *Rivers v. Gulf Canada Ltd.*, 1986 CarswellOnt 845, 13 C.C.E.L. 131 (Ont. H.C.) at p. 139 [C.C.E.L.].

the advice of actuaries which can dramatically increase the costs of a wrongful dismissal action. Since the court decision will typically be given after the notice period has ended, it can only be remedied through a monetary payment with the intention of putting the employee in the position he or she would have been in had he or she been provided with proper notice. The courts are somewhat constrained in the nature of the award they may grant and are not able to reinstate the employee into the pension plan.

Mediated resolution

Where mediation occurs at an early stage, the parties may have many opportunities available to them in regard to pension issues that would not be allowable through a court award. For instance, if the parties agree to structure a settlement as a salary continuance, in which case the employee technically remains on the company payroll, the employee may also be continued as a member of the company's pension plan to the end of the applicable notice period, to the extent that this is permitted by the terms of the pension plan. By allowing the employee to accrue pension credits throughout the notice period, the cost to the employer may be less than what would be awarded by a court, as the employer would have to make a potentially large lump sum payment to compensate the employee for this loss. It may also allow the parties to avoid the costs of actuarial advice. Generally speaking, where a mediated settlement provides an employee with a lump sum payment (*i.e.*, retiring allowance), he or she will not be permitted to remain a participating member of the pension plan.

Where the terminated employee is close to the age of retirement, the parties may also have the flexibility in a mediated solution to bridge the payments in order to allow the employee to continue to participate in the pension plan for a period that may be longer than the reasonable notice period so that they can comply with the requirement of the pension plan. For instance, consider the case of an employee who is entitled to a notice period of 20 months and has been terminated a mere 30 months prior to his normal retirement date. The employee may wish to have the severance payments extended until his normal retirement date. The parties could agree to bridge the 20-month notice period at a lower monthly rate over a period of 30 months in order that the employee can continue to accrue

---

[5] *Dey v. Valley Forest Products Ltd.*, 1994 CarswellNB 182, 151 N.B.R. (2d) 344, 6 C.C.E.L. (2d) 90 (N.B. Q.B.), affirmed 1995 CarswellNB 39, 162 N.B.R. (2d) 207, 11 C.C.E.L. (2d) 1 (N.B. C.A.).

normal pension benefits and ultimately be entitled to regular pension income at the end of that 30-month period.[6] These are the kind of solutions that would not be available to the parties through a court decision. A claim for pension losses is another factor that will be of much greater interest to some employees than to others. In fact, the vast majority of private sector employees do not even participate in pension plans. Some employers provide for RRSP matching programs and profit-sharing plans. The same general principles apply to those plans as to pension plans. Obviously, those employees who are close to their retirement date and have a substantial length of service with the company will be most interested in preserving these pension rights.

(d) Overtime and Vacation Pay

Court award

Employers are required to provide employees with vacation pay accruals during the statutory notice period. The same principle does not likely apply with respect to vacation accruals during the reasonable notice period. Some older decisions have supported a vacation accrual during the reasonable notice period, but the better view is that such accruals are not appropriate. A court will therefore likely just include in its award compensation for vacation accruals during the statutory notice period. Often, an employee claims entitlement to substantial unused vacation time and/or overtime pay that has accrued over the period of employment. Where records have been adequately maintained and there is no express provision that would exclude an employee's entitlement to accrued and unused entitlements, a court may award these items to an employee. However, these payments would be payable as wages and accordingly would be subject to all of the regular payroll deductions including income tax, Canada Pension Plan and Employment Insurance premiums.

Mediated resolution

Where an employee presents a claim for substantial vacation and/or overtime entitlements following the termination of employment, these claims are quite often disputed by the employer. The employer may take the position that it has an established policy that unused vacation time at the end of an applicable year is revoked. The employer may also deny an

---

[6] See Appendices 7A, 7B and 7C for draft letters/mediation documents.

employee's entitlement to overtime pay on a number of other bases. For instance, it may dispute the employee's records or may assert that the employee is not entitled to overtime pay because the position he or she held with the employer was exempt from overtime pay. At mediation, the parties may be willing to make some concessions on these points and may use these items as trading cards. For instance, they may agree to a greater notice period in exchange for the employee's withdrawal of such overtime or vacation pay claims. Because of different characterizations from a tax perspective, it may be beneficial to an employee to fold these amounts into a greater notice period. The employee may also have eligible space in his or her RRSP where part or all of the severance amount may be transferred on a tax deferred basis and this may brighten the offer for the employee.

(e) Bonus Payments

<u>Court award</u>

Generally speaking, a court will award bonus payments to an employee on a *pro rata* basis for the applicable notice period where it is determined that bonus entitlements had been an integral part of the employee's remuneration package with the employer.[7] Courts will also award bonus payments to employees for the current year to the date of termination, on a *pro rata* basis. Employers often try to avoid such awards by arguing that bonuses are payable to eligible employees on a purely discretionary basis and that the employee in question would not have been entitled to a bonus had his or her employment continued in the normal course. Where the employee was terminated for reasons of performance (whether for cause or not), the employer will certainly take the position that the employee would not be entitled to a discretionary bonus and in fact, a court may concur.

<u>Mediated resolution</u>

Entitlements to bonus payments are often very contentious issues at mediation. Many employers are leery of setting precedents with respect to the payment of bonus entitlements to employees following termination, and there may therefore be a substantial incentive to the employer to resolve these issues through mediation. For instance, some employers,

---

[7] *Stewart v. British Columbia Sugar Refinery Co.*, 1994 CarswellMan 115, 2 C.C.E.L. (2d) 125, [1994] 4 W.W.R. 695, 91 Man. R. (2d) 177 (Man. Q.B.) at pp. 131-2 [C.C.E.L.].

particularly those in certain industries such as the investment business, have established policies that preclude an employee from receiving a bonus unless the employee is actively employed with the company at the time of the company's year end. A court decision that grants an employee a bonus on a *pro rata* basis for the part of the year in which he or she worked could be perceived by the employer as a very costly precedent of which it may want to avoid. The confidentiality of both the mediation process and the settlement would allow the parties to resolve this matter and avoid setting such precedents. A bonus awarded by a judge is likely to be an "all or nothing" payment, whereas at mediation, the parties can weigh the risks and make necessary concessions to arrive at a mutually acceptable bonus figure. The parties may also have the flexibility to trade off this item in lieu of a greater notice period or other claims. The parties may also agree to pay the bonus in installments or over a period of more than one tax year, as that is the way they may have received the bonus had it been paid in the normal course of the employment relationship and this arrangement could be beneficial to both parties. Clearly, the parties may each derive benefits from structuring the payments in creative manners.

(f) Stock Options

Court award

Courts have been inclined to award to an employee compensation for loss of stock options during the applicable notice period. The Ontario Court of Appeal has held that unless the terms of the stock option plan clearly and unequivocally state that no options may be exercised beyond the date of termination, employees should be entitled to exercise all options that accrue during the notice period.[8] Since the period of notice will likely have ended by the date of the court's award, an employer may be ordered to compensate the employee for the value of the stock options that the employee would otherwise have been able to exercise (*i.e.*, the difference between the highest stock price since the date of vesting and the strike price). Where the stock price has dramatically increased, this can prove to be very costly for the employer and may also set a precedent that the employer would prefer to avoid. Where markets have been volatile,

---

[8] *Veer v. Dover Corp. (Canada) Ltd./Société Dover (Canada) Ltée*, 1999 CarswellOnt 1466, 2 B.L.R. (3d) 234, 45 C.C.E.L. (2d) 183, 22 C.C.P.B. 119, (sub nom. *Veer v. Dover Corp. (Canada) Ltd.*) 99 C.L.L.C. 210-037, 120 O.A.C. 394 (Ont. C.A.).

valuation can also be a difficult determination as the court would have to determine an appropriate valuation date.

Mediated resolution

At mediation, the parties will retain much more flexibility in the manner in which the issues surrounding stock options can be resolved than they would through a court award. Where options are of substantial value, the employee may even be willing to concede all other claims that he or she has against the company if the company is willing to extend the period in which he or she may exercise stock options. This possibility may of course be limited by the terms of the stock option plan and the requirements of regulatory bodies. Where a number of options will vest outside of the notice period, the parties may bridge the salary payments in order to maintain the employee on payroll for the required period of time so as to allow the employee to exercise the options that would vest. Options are another item that may be strategically used by the parties as trading cards. This claim may be perceived as of greater importance to some employees than to others. The importance of this item will obviously depend on the potential value of the stock options at the relevant time.

(g)   Car Allowance

Court award

A court may award an employee with the value of the loss of the personal use of a company car as well as insurance benefits for the period of reasonable notice.[9] An employee may also be awarded damages for a car allowance which would have been enjoyed by the employee in his or her personal capacity during the notice period.[10]

Mediated resolution

Through mediation, the parties may be able to find more creative solutions to the employee's claim for the loss of a car allowance or company car. Where the employee had the use of a company vehicle, the company may allow the employee to purchase the vehicle at a preferred

---

[9]   *McFadden v. 481782 Ontario Ltd.*, 1984 CarswellOnt 106, 47 O.R. (2d) 134, 27 B.L.R. 173, 5 C.C.E.L. 83 (Ont. H.C.) at p. 94 [C.C.E.L.].

[10]   *Sawko v. Foseco Canada Ltd.*, 1987 CarswellOnt 887, 15 C.C.E.L. 309 (Ont. Dist. Ct.) at p. 316 [C.C.E.L.].

value, such as at the book value. This is a benefit to both parties that would not be available through a court award. The parties could also agree to allow the employee to retain the use of the vehicle for a reasonable period of time until other arrangements can be made by the employee. The parties may have the flexibility to make this period either longer or shorter than the reasonable notice period. The court is only able to award monetary damages that would correspond to the length of the notice period. In many cases, monetary damages may not be as valuable to an employee as would the continued use of the vehicle. As with most other factors, car allowances are something that can certainly be used by each party as a valuable trading card depending on the relative importance of the value of the item.

(h) Mitigation Expenses

Court award

A court will normally award an employee with reasonable expenses incurred by the employee in his or her attempt to find alternate employment during the period of reasonable notice. However, any mitigation expenses that accrue after the notice period are not normally recoverable through a court award.

Mediated resolution

In most wrongful dismissal actions, mitigation expenses are not a large component of the employee's claim. They are generally only significant when an employee incurs extensive travel expenses in pursuit of alternate employment and/or is required to relocate to another community and incurs substantial moving costs as well as losses and expenses associated with the sale of the employee's home. Sometimes an employee only relocates after the completion of a reasonable notice period, especially where that notice period is quite short, and may still seek some compensation for the expenses incurred by the relocation. An employee who faces an expensive relocation as a result of a termination may be willing to trade off other items in order to be reimbursed for the relocation expenses. These expenses may be reimbursed in a more tax-advantageous manner. For instance, a company may agree to pay for the capital loss on a home and this may be tax advantageous to the employee. A court may not, however, be inclined to grant such an award.

(i) Punitive Damages

Court award

In recent years, the courts have been increasingly inclined to award punitive damages to employees in wrongful dismissal actions. Punitive damages are not intended to compensate an employee for a specific loss but they serve the function of punishing and deterring employers from reprehensible or harsh conduct towards an employee. Punitive damages may be awarded by a court where the termination was particularly insensitive, egregious and harsh. For instance, punitive damages may be awarded where an employer has maintained baseless theft or fraud allegations against an employee to the date of trial. In one case, the employee was awarded $10,000 for punitive damages at trial and this award was increased on appeal to $50,000 in order to properly give effect to the purposes of punitive damages of punishment and deterrence.[11] Similarly, in another case, the Ontario Court of Appeal increased an award of punitive damages from $14,000 to $40,000.[12] This was held to be proper law by the Ontario Court of Appeal in *Hobbs v. TDI Canada Ltd.*,[13] but it was distinguished from a divergent line of cases represented by the Supreme Court of Canada in *Maguire v. Northland Drug Co.*[14] Although there does seem to be an increasing acceptance by the courts of the overriding principle of punishment and deterrence, the conduct of the employer must be very harsh in order to meet the threshold required for a court to award punitive damages.

Mediated resolution

A claim by an employee for punitive damages is one that can easily be used as a trading card by the parties. Where the manner of the termination or conduct of the employer is harsh, the employer will likely be fearful of an adverse finding at trial. An adverse ruling may engender very negative publicity for the employer, the impact of which can be very far-reaching to the company's business relationships, business operations, productivity, and employee morale.

---

[11]   *Ribeiro v. Canadian Imperial Bank of Commerce*, 1992 CarswellOnt 964, 13 O.R. (3d) 278, 44 C.C.E.L. 165 (Ont. C.A.), leave to appeal refused (1993), 65 O.A.C. 79 (note), 157 N.R. 400 (note) (S.C.C.).

[12]   *Francis v. Canadian Imperial Bank of Commerce*, 1994 CarswellOnt 995, 21 O.R. (3d) 75, 7 C.C.E.L. (2d) 1, 120 D.L.R. (4th) 393, 95 C.L.L.C. 210-022, 75 O.A.C. 216 (Ont. C.A.).

[13]   2004 CarswellOnt 4989, 37 C.C.E.L. (3d) 163, 246 D.L.R. (4th) 43 (Ont. C.A.), additional reasons 2005 CarswellOnt 818 (Ont. C.A.).

[14]   1935 CarswellMan 94, [1935] S.C.R. 412 (S.C.C.).

On the other hand, sometimes claims of this nature are ones that the employee can use to his or her advantage at a mediation. Although an employer is unlikely to admit that its conduct warrants an award of punitive damages, it may be inclined to increase the period of reasonable notice or grant an employee other tangible assistance in exchange for the employee's agreement to drop these claims. Where the allegations involve issues of human rights, the parties may agree to allocate a portion of the settlement funds to general damages which, if reasonable and appropriate in the circumstances, may be payable without tax implications.

(j) Mental Distress

Court award

On occasion, courts will grant awards to terminated employees for mental distress. The act of dismissal itself (*i.e.*, a straightforward dismissal) is not enough to engender an award of damages for mental distress. If the employer has acted in a business-like manner in conducting the termination, damages for mental distress will not normally be awarded. However, where the termination results in physical symptoms or medically documented symptoms, the courts will be more inclined to make an award for mental distress. The employee will have to prove he or she has been mentally distressed and real, tangible expenses must be presented to the court by the party making the claim. The onus will also rest on the employee to prove that the mental distress flowed from the lack of reasonable notice, the deficiencies in the separation package or the egregious conduct on the part of the employer rather than the fact of dismissal itself.

Mediated resolution

Similar to a claim for punitive damages, an employer is unlikely to admit that it has caused an employee mental distress and will most often be unwilling to allocate any damages to this head of damage. Mediation does, however, provide the parties with an opportunity to develop creative solutions to these claims. At mediation, an employee will be provided with an opportunity to express the particulars of his or her suffering as a result of the termination. Sometimes, a simple apology by the employer to an employee will suffice in resolving this claim. However, this simple solution cannot be awarded by a court. In addition, the parties may be able to structure other creative solutions such as having the employer pay for the cost of therapy sessions to assist with the treatment of an employee and/or providing relocation counselling to assist with the employee's pursuit of new employment. In appropriate circumstances, which are medically documented, the parties may even agree to place the employee on short- or long-term disability until the employee is no longer disabled and is ready to return to the workforce. Without admitting liability, the employer can take positive and compassionate steps to assist a former employee to regain the proper balance following a difficult termination experience. Where claims of this nature are made, the parties may be able to appropriately allocate a portion of the settlement to "general damages".

(k) Disability Claims

Court award

Disability claims are ones that may arise either in the context of a wrongful dismissal suit or separate and apart from a wrongful dismissal action. Claims for disability benefits are generally brought against a third party insurer rather than the employer itself, although the employer may be implicated in the matter for various reasons. Generally, where the individual is able to establish for the court that he or she is totally disabled from employment, and the employee was covered under a disability plan at the time of the onset of disability, the court will make an award for damages. The damage award will constitute a retroactive payment to the date of the onset of the disability plus interest on those payments. Where there is a finding that the employee is currently totally disabled from employment, the insured company should reinstate the employee to benefits until such time that he or she no longer meets the criteria required to satisfy the definition of disability. Where the employer is also involved in the action, there may be a damage award against the employer for loss of pension or other benefits to the employee for the disputed period of time. Where the employer failed to properly continue the employee on disability benefits following termination, the employer rather than the insurance company can be held liable for disability income. In these situations, the employer effectively becomes the employee's disability insurer.

Mediated resolution

Disability claims are well-suited to mediation. Insurance companies are often eager to avoid legal precedents and the significant costs associated with litigating disability matters. Through early mediation, the

150

parties may be able to develop creative solutions to the dispute and may be able to do so without the need for extensive and costly medical assessments and medical opinions, which would be required in a court proceeding. Depending on the nature of the disability and the prognosis, the individual may be most interested in a reinstatement of benefits. However, if his or her prognosis is good, he or she may be more interested in a retroactive damage claim with some small future damage component. Mediation allows the parties to structure the settlement in a variety of ways that suits their mutual interests. It also allows the individual to express his or her feelings and emotions about the issues which may, in turn, facilitate an early resolution. The parties may also agree to additional terms such as payment of special treatments that might not otherwise be covered pursuant to the policy of insurance.

(l) Costs and Interest

Court award

If a matter proceeds to court, the successful party may be entitled to reimbursement by the other party of a portion of legal fees. Rarely, however, will the cost award be equal to the actual legal fees incurred by the party. Where an employee receives an award of damages, he or she will also be entitled to both pre- and post-judgment interest on the award at rates prescribed by the courts.

Mediated resolution

Where parties are successful at resolving a dispute at a mediation, costs often form part of the settlement. The employer often agrees to pay either all or a portion of the employee's legal fees incurred as a result of the dispute. Sometimes, an employee will be willing to accept a significantly lower damage award if his or her total legal fees are covered by the employer. The employer, on the other hand, may be reluctant, on principle, to pay the employee's legal costs. This is often a very important trading card used by the parties in an employment law mediation. Where the parties are able to settle a dispute, they will often agree to an appropriate allocation for pre-judgment interest. Through a mediated settlement, the parties may merely allocate an acceptable portion of the agreed upon sum to interest, rather than paying an amount over and above the settlement. It merely allows the party greater flexibility in terms of allocating the funds than they would be permitted through a court award.

3. HUMAN RIGHTS DISPUTES

Although there are obvious benefits to resolving human rights disputes through mediation rather than proceeding through the standard hearing process of the human rights body, there may not be a significant difference in the nature of the remedies available through a mediated solution versus a decision of a human rights adjudicator. That is because an adjudicator has much wider scope to provide creative remedies than does a court in a civil action. As will be discussed in Chapter 8, "Special Issues in Mediating Employment Law Disputes", an adjudicator may grant a variety of awards including reinstatement of an employee to the same or a different position within the company, an apology, damages, back wages, future loss of income and letter of reference. It may also grant awards on a public policy basis which provide broad remedies such as the implementation of employment policies and training programs by the employer.

Mediation may allow the parties to structure these items in the most beneficial ways. Since the employer may be eager to avoid an intrusive hearing process and negative publicity and as the employee may also wish to close this chapter of his or her life, there are many trading cards that each party can use to reach the most mutually beneficial resolution. The parties will also have control over the nature of the remedy. Perhaps an employee who has been subjected to sexual harassment at the hands of her manager is not interested in returning to her employment. A hearing may not permit the same level of frankness between the parties and may result in an outcome that neither party finds particularly desirable.

4. INTERNAL EMPLOYMENT DISPUTES — "WORKPLACE MEDIATIONS"

As discussed in Chapter 2, "Determining When to Mediate", mediation of internal employment disputes can be very useful and allow for much greater creativity and proactive solutions than would be allowed if the matter festered and eventually culminated in a wrongful dismissal action. Through early mediation of these disputes, the parties may be able to create proactive resolutions to problems that may actually prove to be quite simple if addressed at an early stage. Where an employee is encountering a personality dispute with a supervisor or co-worker, mediation may allow the parties to discuss their concerns and either clear the air between them or develop methods by which they will interact. This could mean agreeing that all work-related interaction between them will be through e-mail correspondence or alternatively, identifying a neutral person whom either party may speak to in the event an issue develops between them. Where an employee is dissatisfied with the result of a performance appraisal, through mediation, the employee and his or her supervisor may be successful at addressing the areas of disagreement and setting mutually agreeable standards for future performance. The kinds of remedies available through a workplace mediation are limitless and can serve to salvage a quickly deteriorating employment relationship. Without use of a "workplace mediation", the employer may have otherwise simply terminated an employee involved in a conflict, which in many cases, would not be the most desirable result and could lead to unnecessary and costly litigation.

APPENDIX 7A
TERMINATION LETTER

Ms. Jane Smith
123 Elm Street
Toronto, ON
M5R 1Z4

Dear Ms. Smith:

Further to our discussions, this will confirm that as a result of a restructuring of our organization, your employment will be terminated effective immediately.

In recognition of your lengthy years of service with the company, the company is prepared to provide you with the following severance package in exchange for an executed release in the form attached:

1. Lump sum payment equivalent to 18 months' salary inclusive of your entitlements pursuant to the *Employment Standards Act*.
2. Continuation of employee benefits excluding pension and STD and LTD for a period of 18 months. Pension, STD and LTD will be continued for the eight-week statutory notice period.
3. Outplacement counselling for a period of six months to assist you in your job search.
4. Positive letter of reference.

Would you please provide us with the executed release within seven days of today's date. We regret that this decision was necessary and wish you well in your future endeavour.

Yours very truly,
Robert Boss

APPENDIX 7B

DEMAND LETTER

Mr. Robert Boss
ABC Inc.
50 Smith Street
Toronto, ON
M6T 8Y2

Dear Mr. Boss:

RE: Ms. Jane Smith

We have been retained by Ms. Jane Smith with respect to the recent termination of her employment from ABC Inc.

As you know, Ms. Smith worked for your organization for a period of 25 years, most recently in the role of Manager, Logistics. In that role, she earned an annual income in the amount of $75,000 and was entitled to assorted employee benefits as well as participation in the company's pension plan.

The company's decision to terminate Ms. Smith's employment at this point in her career, just 30 months from her early retirement date seems harsh. It will be very difficult for Ms. Smith to obtain new employment in view of her age and proximity to retirement.

It is our view that a court would clearly award Ms. Smith notice in an amount no less than 24 months and would not only continue her employee benefits for this period, but would also award her an amount for the loss of her pension benefit for this period.

It is our view that the following offer would be appropriate:

1. Salary continuance for a period of 24 months.
2. Benefit continuation for a period of 24 months and continuation in the pension plan for this period.
3. Outplacement counselling at a reputable firm.
4. Positive letter of reference.

May we please hear from you by no later than seven days from the date of this letter.

Yours very truly,
Jay Litigator

APPENDIX 7C
MINUTES OF SETTLEMENT

BETWEEN:

Jane Smith

(the "Employee")

– and –

ABC Inc.

(the "Company")

Whereas the Employee's employment was terminated effective July 2, 2011; and

Whereas the Employee's early retirement date is January 1, 2014;

The parties hereby agree to settle all issues between them on the following basis:

1. The company will continue the Employee's salary for a period of 30 months from July 2, 2011 until January 1, 2014. The company will provide the Employee with a monthly payment on the last business day of each month in the amount of $5,000.00 less required statutory deductions. (The salary continuance is premised on the basis of a 20-month payment which is bridged over a period of 30 months.)
2. The company will continue the Employee's benefits until January 1, 2014, at which time the Employee will become entitled to retiree benefits.
3. The Employee will remain a participant in the pension plan until January 1, 2014, and both the Employee and Company will make the regular contributions thereto.
4. The Company will contribute the sum of $5,000 plus HST towards the Employee's legal fees.

5.   The Employee will execute a full and final release in the form attached hereto.

Agreed to this_____day of_____, 2012.

_____
Witness

Jane Smith
Per: ABC Inc.

Chapter 8

SPECIAL ISSUES IN MEDIATING EMPLOYMENT LAW DISPUTES

1. OVERVIEW

There are specific characteristics of some employment law disputes that can create unique issues and challenges for the parties, their counsel and the mediator. For example, mediations conducted through human rights bodies are somewhat different than "private mediations" and we will discuss the special characteristics of these sorts of mediations in some detail. Some employment mediations involve multiple parties which often lead to substantially different interpersonal dynamics than mediations where only two parties are involved. It is also not uncommon in employment law mediations to encounter substantial power imbalances between the parties. Furthermore, where extreme acrimony exists between the parties, the mediation process may be hindered. This chapter will canvass these issues and provide you with some guidance on how best to deal with these unique and challenging circumstances.

2. HUMAN RIGHTS MEDIATIONS

The Ontario Human Rights Tribunal introduced mediation as a mechanism for resolving human rights complaints in May 1997. The mandate of the tribunal is to provide parties to a dispute with the option of resolving their complaints at a much earlier stage in the complaint process than would otherwise be available to them. The process is offered to parties of a human rights dispute immediately upon receipt of the complaint. Through a hearing process, an adjudicator looks at the concerns, hears the evidence and makes a decision, unless the complaint is resolved through mediation. An adjudicator has very broad authority in the nature of the award he or she may grant. For instance, the adjudicator may award damages for loss of income as well as damages for mental distress or pain and suffering. The adjudicator may also reinstate an employee who has been terminated from his or her employment as a result of discriminatory conduct and the adjudicator may order specific proactive steps on the part of the respondents. This may include providing an apology and establishing policies and training programs to ensure a discriminatory-free workplace. A decision by an adjudicator will also be a public document which has the potential to cause embarrassment to the employer and the individual respondents. It is not difficult to see why the implementation of the mediation process by the tribunal has had broad appeal to all parties and significant impact on the conduct and the resolution of human rights complaints in Ontario. In 2012, the Attorney General of Ontario commissioned Andrew Pinto to conduct a review of the tribunal. It was determined that just under one-half of new applications received by the tribunal each year proceeded to mediation and that approximately 65 percent of those were resolved at mediation. It was recommended that the tribunal dedicate more resources and determine means by which mediation can occur as early as possible after the receipt of a response.[1]

The majority of human rights cases involve matters of employment and accordingly, the mediation process through the Human Rights Tribunal has had substantial impact on the practice of human rights/ employment law.[2] A large number of employment-related human rights disputes proceed to mediation. It seems that regardless of whether the party is a complainant or a respondent, human rights issues are ones that many parties will see great merit in resolving as quickly and amicably as possible. Even where the respondents see no validity to a complainant's complaint, the concern of having an unresolved human rights complaint hanging over them may seem particularly overwhelming and stressful to individual respondents and in the case of corporate respondents, it may be deemed as contrary to business interests. They may also be motivated to avoid a full hearing before an adjudicator and the embarrassment that an adverse ruling may cause. Those employers who rely on public funding may feel particularly vulnerable when human rights complaints are pursued against them as it can jeopardize their continued public funding.

Similar to the process involved in both private and mandatory mediations, in human rights mediations, the parties are required to sign a mediation agreement that ensures the confidentiality of the process. Any information disclosed through the mediation process cannot be used in the subsequent tribunal hearing.

---

[1]   *Report of the Ontario Human Rights Review 2012*, Andrew Pinto, submitted to the Honourable John Gerritsen, Attorney General of Ontario, November 2012.
[2]   *A Guide to Mediation Services* (Toronto: Queen's Printer, Government of Ontario, 1997).

One factor that is often of significant importance to the Human Rights Tribunal is the public interest mandate. For obvious reasons, complaints of discrimination involve issues of public interest. For instance, if a company is discriminating against employees on the basis of age by terminating only its older employees and retaining younger employees with the same or lower level of skills, there are broad public interest implications. Although there may be individual remedies available to an employee who files a complaint on this basis, there may be other broader remedies that must be invoked to ensure that the company's discriminatory conduct is rectified. Generally, mediations conducted through the Human Rights Tribunal will take place on the neutral grounds of the human rights office located nearest to the parties. The meetings are usually conducted on a face-to-face basis. It may also proceed through telephone conference calls where the geographic distance between the parties makes meeting face-to-face either difficult or costly. It is also not uncommon to proceed through a shuttle mediation process whereby the mediator works with each party individually and goes back and forth between them to convey their respective positions.

Like any other employment law matter, the mediator is a neutral third party who works with the parties to facilitate an acceptable resolution. The mediators used by the tribunal have experience in dealing with the unique circumstances and party characteristics that are often found in human rights complaints.

It is our view that the implementation of mediation services by the Human Rights Tribunal has been a very worthwhile endeavour to resolve employment-related human rights complaints. These human rights matters may not be as effectively dealt with through private mediation because private mediators may not be as equipped to deal with the unique and sensitive issues that are often raised in human rights complaints. Where there are additional issues beyond the human rights complaint itself, these may also be dealt with effectively at the human rights mediation. The parties may be able to reach a global resolution with respect to all issues between them.

3. DEALING WITH POWER IMBALANCES

Facing power imbalances in a mediation can be a very serious obstacle to obtaining a satisfactory and fair result. Any result that is achieved may strongly favour more powerful parties. There may be an inherent power imbalance by virtue of the nature of some relationships. For instance, an employee may feel a substantial power deficit in relation to his or her powerful, large and deep-pocketed employer. A victim of sexual harassment may feel a substantial power deficit in relation to the alleged accused who may be the victim's supervisor or manager. He or she may also feel substantially weaker than the employer from whom the employee may obtain little support.

Power imbalances may also surface unexpectedly during the course of a mediation session, where one of the parties is either overpowering the other or one party is being disempowered. Where this becomes apparent, counsel for the disempowered party must take steps to protect his or her client's interest and the mediator must develop strategies to alleviate these problems, without compromising his or her neutrality.

Unfortunately, unlike a judge or adjudicator, a mediator does not have the authority to order the disclosure of relevant documentation or information that may assist the vulnerable party. In fact, the mediator does not have any direct power to address the power imbalance.

Where power imbalances are a concern, the mediator may separate the parties and utilize the shuttle mediation technique, which involves the mediator going back and forth between the parties. For instance, in a race discrimination case, the victim of discrimination may experience overwhelming anxiety if he or she is forced to sit in the same room as the alleged accused. He or she may be unable to communicate his or her interests while experiencing this high level of anxiety. It may be determined that both parties would be best served by remaining separated throughout the mediation process.

Where the power imbalance cannot be remedied during the course of a mediation and there is concern that any resolution reached would be unfair and unbalanced, it is sometimes prudent for the disempowered party to discontinue the mediation and proceed through the litigation process where power imbalances should have less of a negative impact. Litigation may be a disempowered party's best protection against an abuse of power. However, it is generally accepted that where the weaker party understands the nature of the process as well as its constraints, he or she should not be discouraged from participating in the mediation process.

Prior to entering the mediation room, you as counsel should clearly apprise your client about the concern of power imbalances, whether you are acting for the powerful or potentially disempowered party. If a weaker party is prepared for the stronger party's actions, he or she may be able to confront them with little difficulty. Through proper preparation of your client as well as strong negotiation skills on your part, your client may be well protected from an abuse of power. An individual may also feel more empowered if the individual includes his or her spouse or other close friend or relative in the proceedings. By considering these issues in advance of the mediation, you can take steps to protect or shield your client from these problems.

As counsel in an employment law matter, you may sometimes find yourself facing an unrepresented litigant. Counsel has an ethical duty to remain fair and operate with candour. Counsel should identify issues and rigorously inform self-represented parties of obligations prior to any important dates. It is best to use email and correspondence rather than telephone calls or voice mail for such matters. Counsel will have to consider whether mediation will work with an unrepresented litigant as sometimes they will not consider a settlement that is less than their claimed amount. There may also be a tendency for the mediator to assist an unrepresented party so that they can make informed settlement decisions.

4. DEALING WITH PUBLIC INTEREST ISSUES

Broad public interest issues are often easy to identify in matters involving human rights. For instance, where an employer requires employees of a defined religious group to work on their religious holidays, the actions of the employer may be deemed discriminatory, even though unintentional in nature. In another example, where an employer allows employees to post sexually suggestive pictures in the workplace, the company's inaction may be deemed discriminatory to women and conducive to a poisoned work atmosphere. The scope and the impact of these issues are much broader than those of the employees at each of these workplaces who are directly impacted by the company's actions or inactions. They impact society as a whole. A determination of these issues will espouse societal norms and act as a standard for future community behaviour. A decision by a court or tribunal will not only provide a remedy for the case at hand but it will also provide important legal precedents for employers as a whole to follow and adhere to.

Although mediation has numerous benefits and can provide a satisfactory remedy for the parties to the dispute, it may deprive the broader community of an appropriate remedy. Because of the necessary confidentiality of the process and the lack of a reported decision, the mediation process does not establish any legal precedents and its results are in no way binding on any individuals who are not parties to the dispute. That is why some cases with a significant public interest component to the dispute are simply not suitable for mediation.

In human rights mediations, the public interest concerns may become part of a satisfactory resolution. For instance, in the second example provided above, even though only one female employee may complain that the employer has allowed inappropriate pictures to be displayed in the workplace, a satisfactory resolution may require more than a remedy to the complainant alone. An effective resolution would require the company to not only cease such conduct, but may also require the company to take steps such as submitting an apology to all staff and establishing a harassment policy with extensive training for all staff. This remedy would clearly go beyond remedying the impact that the infraction had on the complainant. It would seek to remedy potential future infractions as well as the poisoned work atmosphere and it would serve to educate the employer and the workforce as a whole. When providing its approval to a mediated settlement, this is likely the nature of the settlement with broad public interest components that the Human Rights Tribunal would wish to see.

5. DEALING WITH MULTIPLE PARTIES

The interpersonal dynamics of a mediation will certainly be different when more than two parties are involved in the dispute. Where there are three or more parties, one party's interest may be more divergent from some of the parties than from others. In the majority of employment cases, there will be only one complainant or plaintiff (typically the employee) but there may be several defendants or respondents. Often, the defendants will have similar interests, although they will not always share identical interests. Where their interests are similar in nature, they may choose to be represented by the same counsel. With the exception of human rights complaints where the employer may not stand behind the actions of an accused employee or manager, employers do most often support the actions of their managers who may be implicated in the dispute along with the employer and they will often be represented by the same counsel. In many cases, the employer will be vicariously liable for the actions of the manager if the actions were carried out in the course of the manager's employment. Where the defendants are represented by the same counsel and their interests are similar, the mediation may not proceed in a substantially different manner than it would where there existed only one defendant. However, the overall mediation process may be more time-consuming as there are more parties to be heard and more parties with whom to reach a consensus.

164

Where the defendants are represented by different counsel as a result of their distinct or divergent interests, the mediation process may become much more complicated. Not only will the mediation process likely take much longer, but finding middle ground for a satisfactory resolution for all parties may become much more difficult. Power imbalances may also be more significant. Some parties may become more guarded and/or anxious when there are multiple parties involved in the dispute. It may be necessary to separate the parties throughout the mediation process to account for some of these potential difficulties. Managing these issues can be challenging for a mediator and it is wise to select an experienced mediator for a multi-party mediation. It may also be a case where co-mediation will be desirable.

As discussed in Chapter 5, "The Role of Counsel", counsel who represents more than one party should make it very clear to his or her clients that potential conflicts could develop and the clients should be well aware of their ongoing right to retain independent counsel. Counsel should also be wary of these issues throughout the mediation and quickly identify conflicts that develop during the mediation process. On occasion, it may be necessary to halt the mediation in order to allow the parties to each obtain their own counsel.

It may also become apparent to one or more of the parties during a mediation process that a necessary party has not been included in the proceeding. Information may be brought forward that makes it clear that there are further potential defendants in this matter. For instance, a case involving a disabled employee may not be confined to issues between just the employee and his or her employer. It may become apparent that the disability insurer should also be included in the dispute. It may be necessary to halt the mediation until further information can be gathered and/or a claim can be amended to include the insurance company as a party in the dispute. In a further example, a company that has sued a former employee for breach of restrictive covenants and loss of business revenues as a result of these breaches may determine that the employee's new employer should also be included in the action. Where mediation is conducted at a very early stage in a proceeding, these issues will often not become apparent until mediation is underway and the parties have learned more about each other's case. Although usually the opposite is true, sometimes a case that at first appears quite simple will become more complex as it proceeds.

The defendants may also realize during the course of a mediation that third parties should be included in the dispute which may impact that defendant's own liability.

Multiple parties in employment mediations are commonly found in human rights disputes, sexual harassment disputes and disability matters. Multiple parties may also be found in wrongful dismissal disputes where there are independent actions against employees or managers of the company. The vast majority of wrongful dismissal claims, however, will just involve the employee and his or her former employer.

In an internal "workplace mediation", the number of parties can range from two to several. If the matter involves bullying or a poisoned work atmosphere, there may be several respondents in addition to the employer. They all may need to be involved in the mediation process to allow for a comprehensive and fulsome resolution.

6. DEALING WITH SIGNIFICANT ACRIMONY BETWEEN THE PARTIES

In many employment law disputes, there will be a substantial level of acrimony between the parties. This is not surprising considering that it is often from an employment relationship that an individual derives his or her feelings of self-worth, self-respect and self-esteem. Where these have been hampered by the perceived actions of the employer, an employee may feel distrust and anger towards the employer. They may also suffer extreme anxiety. Although some level of acrimony is considered normal and is in fact expected in an employment dispute, where it is extreme, the dispute may be better dealt with through a process other than mediation. That is something to be determined by the parties and their respective counsel.[3]

Where mediation does proceed and it becomes apparent that the level of acrimony is substantial, the mediator will need to develop techniques to deal with these potential difficulties. This may require separating the parties and conducting the mediation through a shuttle mediation process. It may be determined that allowing the parties to vent their feelings in the presence of the opponent may prove to be worthwhile as it may serve to clear the air and allow the parties to proceed to resolve the matter in a less anxiety-ridden manner and on clearer terms. It may also be determined that an evaluative mediation may be more effective as it would take some of the control out of the hands of the parties and place greater control in the hands of the mediator. Purely facilitative mediations may not be possible where high levels of acrimony exist between the

---

[3] See Chapter 2, "Determining When to Mediate", for a detailed analysis of when mediation is appropriate.

parties. Where there is substantial acrimony, it may also be helpful to utilize a co-mediation process, as two or more mediators may have greater success at overcoming these hurdles and helping the parties find middle ground.

Where these approaches do not work, one or more of the parties may decide to end the mediation process and proceed through the litigation process or through some other alternative dispute mechanism process.

Chapter 9

THE VIEW FROM THE MEDIATOR'S CHAIR

As we have suggested in this book, no two mediation sessions are alike and neither are the styles and perspectives of two mediators. Each mediator brings a unique style and persona to the mediation room. Although this may sometimes bring about a different result to the legal matter, it will most certainly bring about a different "feel" in the mediation room, depending on who is sitting in the mediator's chair.

We are very fortunate to have received the following excerpts from a few of the preeminent employment mediators in Canada. These excerpts showcase each mediator's perspective about what leads to a good mediation session. We sincerely thank Barry Fisher, Lisa Feld, Steve Raymond and Michael Silver for their time, effort and insight in providing us each with their unique perspective.

Peeling Back the Onion: Getting to a Settlement

Barry B. Fisher

I have been asked by the authors to outline a few of my insights as an employment law mediator as to what makes for a successful mediation. The focus of this paper is how to deal in a mediation with a common tendency among employment disputants (and undoubtedly in other practice areas as well) to exaggerate and inflame the dispute prior to the mediation.

There may be many understandable reasons why this occurs so much in the employment law field, given the importance of the employment relationship in our lives and the affect of ending that relationship. However, the reason for this phenomenon is not the focus of this paper.

There is no doubt in my mind that this expansion of the original dispute has a detrimental effect on the chances of the parties achieving a fair and just resolution of their conflict.

I hope that this paper will contribute to an ongoing discussion of how we can all help resolve employment disputes in a fair and cost effective manner.

1. Peeling Back the Onion

By the time the typical wrongful dismissal action gets to mediation, the parties have often exchanged extensive correspondence and have completed the court pleadings. By the time of the mediation, anywhere from three to eighteen months has passed since the termination.

In many cases, what started out as a simple not for cause dismissal has now morphed into a complex and highly inflammatory set of pleadings in which the plaintiff has alleged not only the failure to provide reasonable notice but also claims damages for mental distress, harassment, discrimination, punitive damages and perhaps reinstatement .

Not to be outdone, the defendant for the first time alleges just cause, a previously forgotten employment contract and an utter failure to mitigate. Increasingly, a counterclaim is thrown in for good measure.

A good mediation brief would either eliminate the more peripheral issues or at least de-emphasize them. Unfortunately, many mediation briefs are nothing more than a reprinting of the pleadings.

The parties show up and expect the mediator to help them resolve all these complex issues in three hours.

171

MEDIATING EMPLOYMENT DISPUTES

Quite often these issues are raised for one or more strategic reasons unrelated to the actual trial of the action. The intention may be to scare the other side into settlement by making large and inflammatory claims. The typical reaction by the party on the receiving end of the threat is to return the threat and raise the ante by adding even more outrageous defenses or additional claims.

However, there may also be a more creative reason for this multiplication of claims. Certain claims may or may not attract different tax consequences. By pleading claims that have a more favourable tax consequence, the parties often seek to change a taxable receipt into a non-taxable receipt.

When faced with this common scenario, I look upon the dispute as if it were an onion. An onion is a great vegetable once it is cleaned up and prepared. First, you have to take the dirt off it, then you take the outer layers off, then you cut it up (which is often a tearful process) and finally you apply heat. At the end you have a useful and nutritious food that goes well with many tasty dishes.

In a mediation I first determine what issues are mere window dressing that I hope neither lawyer really takes seriously. This is the dirt removal stage. I may say to defense counsel, "You are not seriously relying on this 20-year-old employment contract are you?" or "For the purpose of the mediation only, can you agree to 'park' the issue of cause?" On the plaintiff's side, I may say, "Absent any meaningful medical reports, I take it that for today's purposes only, we do not have to dwell too long on your client's claim for mental distress."

Then I try to get agreement on some less important issues that can probably be readily agreed to, for instance the cost of benefits, the provision of a reference letter, or simply an understanding that if we get a deal then it will be a salary continuation arrangement. This is the "peeling off the skin" stage.

The cutting of the onion is the tough part. This is where the mediator works on the parties to be intellectually honest about the strengths and weaknesses of their case or the real issues in the case. If the defendant's allegation of cause depends on the trial evidence of their former CFO, who is presently also suing them, the acknowledgement of this trial reality needs to be discussed and worked into the litigation risk strategy.

If the plaintiff, after 12 months in a 15 to 18-month notice case, has done next to nothing to even pretend to look for a job, the plaintiff needs to realize that this deficiency will probably mean that the court will award a notice period at the lower end of the range.

Finally you are at the stage where both parties are realizing that their case is not airtight and there are real risks if the case is not settled. This is when the mediator, and often the lawyer, applies the heat. Hopefully by this time the parties have made a series of meaningful offers, but there is still a gap before you have a deal. Different cases call for different closing techniques.

There can be the soft sell. This may be telling the small employer that you totally understand how frustrated he must feel to be paying this ex-employee 12 months' termination pay when the Ministry of Labour told him he only had to pay eight weeks. However, he has now learnt that in the future he should call his lawyer before he terminates anyone, so this will probably not happen again.

Then there is the hard sell. The plaintiff may have to be told that no matter what he heard from his brother-in-law the dentist or what he thinks he read on a Web site, there is no way that a Canadian judge is going to award him 36 months' notice, especially after only eight years of employment.

If a deal is reached, we can now enjoy the sweetness of the onion. The defendant gets rid of an aggravating piece of litigation that is tying up his time and the plaintiff can now pay some of his bills. Both parties also have the extra benefit of perhaps not having to see their lawyers again.

2. What is a month worth?

There are often many components of an employee's compensation package. These can include base salary, commission, bonus, health benefits, pension, vacation entitlement and stock options. There is extensive case law and legal analysis in the standard texts as to what is included in the reasonable notice period and how to value it.

I find it very useful to try to get the parties to agree on what a month of notice is worth before you exchange offers. This understanding is ultimately reflected in a monthly dollar amount which represents the value of one month's notice.

I do this for several reasons.

First, it is helpful to have a situation where early on in the mediation the parties have agreed to something. This shows the parties that they can actually agree on the little things so there is some hope that they can later agree on the bigger issues.

173

Secondly, the process of agreeing on a monthly number often involves mutual compromise, again a valuable lesson for the balance of the mediation.

Third, it means that when you are going back and forth with various offers, in so far as those offers are expressed in terms of months of notice, there will be no dispute as to how much six months is worth because you already agreed what one month is worth. This serves to narrow the issues as the mediation goes on and lessens the tendency of one party or the other to revisit issues that have already been agreed upon.

Finally, if the mediation does not result in an overall settlement, the parties can still agree that they have signed off on this issue and agree to only litigate the number of months' notice. This would not only shorten the trial but also relieve the trial judge from doing math, which most of them appreciate.

3. It is all about the number of months of notice

At the end of the day, in most cases the most important monetary issue is the amount of reasonable notice that the court would likely award.

In a non-cause case, the amount of reasonable notice is often the only real issue.

Even in a case involving just cause, limitation of notice pursuant to an employment contract or a failure to mitigate, the quantum of notice is very relevant as each side needs to know what the upside or downside is if these defenses fail. For instance, if the issue is the enforceability of a termination clause in an employment contract, then the difference between the contractual amount and the common law notice period must be understood by all parties so that the correct risk analysis can be applied. If the difference between the contractual severance amount and common law notice was $100,000 the parties may well invest more legal fees and time than if the difference was only $15,000.

There is extensive case law, legal commentary and computer databases on determining the range of reasonable notice. The best a lawyer can advise his or her client on is the likely range of notice periods. No lawyer can say that this particular case is worth exactly 17 months' notice, but they could say that the most likely notice period is between 15 and 18 months.

The determination of the proper notice period is founded on well known legal principles. These principles do **not** include the following factors:

1) What a plaintiff or a defendant thinks is fair.
2) What this employer or any other employer has settled other cases for.
3) The reason for the dismissal where cause is not alleged.
4) The reasonableness by either party of an offer made on a without prejudice basis.
5) Whether the employer is a charity or a commercial enterprise.
6) The belief that there is a simple formula applicable to all cases where the amount of notice is directly related only to the years of service. In other words, a simple rule of thumb.

As a mediator, one of the prime attributes that I look for in counsel acting on behalf of a party is what I call "intellectual honesty". This means that I expect the lawyers not to assume that I just fell off the cabbage truck when it comes to matters like assessing the likely notice period. When I read a defense mediation brief where the lawyer states that the plaintiff's entitlement to common law notice is the same as that set out in the *Employment Standards Act, 2000*,[1] I question whether he or she is just ignorant of the law or whether he or she is writing the brief solely to please his or her client.

It is much more persuasive advocacy to state your honest, or at least your almost honest opinion, in the mediation brief and in the mediation. Surprisingly, if you are bold enough to give an honest assessment, the odds are that so too will your opponent. If you are honest in your opinion and the other side remains silly in theirs, most mediators will work hard to move the sillier party. The truth is that evaluative mediators do not "beat up" both sides equally. In fact I and my mediator colleagues do not "beat up" the reasonable party. We usually reserve these tougher tactics for the more unreasonable party. This, in effect, rewards the more reasonable party, for by being reasonable, you avoid the "wrath" of the mediator.

Therefore, if you come to a mediation with a reasonable position on notice, back up your opinion with objective legal research, and remember that one month of notice up or down is probably worth more than any other single issue, you will likely get a deal that is truly reflective of the legal risk of your case.

---

[1] S.O. 2000, c. 41.

4.   Not every case settles at mediation and that is OK.

Most busy mediators in this field have a pretty good success rate. However, not all cases settle at mediation, nor should they.

Sometimes one side is just trying to bully the other into an unfair deal. Their sole tactic is to intimidate, threaten and talk incessantly about costs. One way to combat these tactics is to keep your case simple. If you are the plaintiff and the case is all about notice, then do not plead all the usual tort claims. If you are a defendant facing a crazed plaintiff, consider unilaterally paying the plaintiff what you believe is the low end of reasonable notice. If the matter comes to court, the reasonable employer often wins against the plaintiff with exaggerated claims.

Often at a mediation new issues arise or new facts come out which may change your perspective on the case. However, you came to the mediation with settlement instructions that did not take into account this new information. Rather than treat the mediation as a failure, thereby depriving yourself of an opportunity to settle, consider continuing the mediation to another date so that you do the necessary research and obtain new settlement instructions.

There are a small percentage of litigants who do not want to settle under any circumstances. They often have underlying psychiatric issues and a complete misunderstanding of the Canadian judicial system. They often do not want to settle because without this dispute in their lives, they would have nothing to live for. Mediation is not generally a useful process for these types of litigants. In fact, when these types of people are plaintiffs, they usually are incapable or unwilling to even make an offer, let alone accept the other party's offer.

Some people, usually ones with money to burn, actually enjoy litigating and do not want to settle because they want the other side to suffer and they simply have to win any fight that they enter. To them, compromise is only for wimps. If they lose at trial they appeal automatically. The monetary cost of losing is less than the psychic joy of the fight. Surprisingly however, this does not mean that they will not settle; they just will not compromise. So if they sue you for $10,000 they will settle for $10,000 but not a dime less. If they are defendants, they may offer a deal that is intended only to partially pay the other party's lawyer. This way the plaintiff gets nothing in his or her pocket and the plaintiff's lawyer probably gets screwed on his or her fees. This pleases the defendant.

However, the most common reason for failure at a mediation in my opinion is what I call the "Wizard of Oz" problem. The true decision-maker is not at the mediation as his or her time is too important to waste on this little matter. However, the absent decision-maker (a.k.a. the Wizard) does not trust his or her lawyer or HR Manager to actually make a decision so he or she provides instructions before the mediation that are largely unburdened by his or her own lawyer's opinion, or by inconvenient facts. Both the lawyer and the HR manager fear the wrath of the Wizard because the lawyer does not want to lose a client, and the HR manager likes having a job, so they will not risk making a recommendation to the Wizard regarding a settlement they know he or she will not like. In other words, the most important job in the world is the one that I have, and I am not going to risk my job to help you get a settlement.

The answer to this dilemma is to have the Wizard attend the mediation in person. A good mediator can have a frank discussion with the Wizard and tell him or her honestly about the case. Wizards are rarely stupid. They usually respond favourably to someone who tells them like it is. Secretly I think they admire the tenacity of the strong mediator. After all, they see themselves as strong and most people like people who are similar to them.

The other advantage of the Wizard's physical attendance at the mediation is that the employee will know that when the Wizard says that this really is his or her final offer, the employee will believe him. Once an employee knows that if he or she does not accept this offer, and they will probably go to trial, the employee will likely take a less than great offer.

What Makes for a Successful Mediation, From the Mediator's Perspective?

Lisa Feld

In my years of experience, it is counsel who views mediation as the most important step in the litigation process.

I see my role as mediator as akin to an improvisational actor. I am never sure who is going to say what, when or how. As a mediator, I am prepared to do whatever it takes to keep the conversation going in a positive, professional and productive manner.

To me, it's simple, my favourite and most successful directors and actors in this active theatre-like adventure are counsel who:

1. Write a great script

As mediators, our first impressions are formed by reading the briefs you send in advance. Repeated pleadings are not the way to tell a great story, and cut and paste jobs are sloppy. Always using the same opening and closing paragraphs in every brief only make you fodder for game show-like antics when we play match the counsel to the paragraph.

Think of the program you read before the play, it is short, succinct, and easy to digest, and it gives you a wonderful snapshot of the plot. It sets you up to enjoy the show. Please tell us an interesting story and give us important facts and details of the case, including settlement discussions to date.

2. Ready to test the script in a preview

What do you mean there has been no discussion between counsel? With all the technology available today to enhance new and fast ways to communicate, why have you not emailed, texted or simply called each other to talk? How are you able to gauge if your thoughts are being understood? It is okay to agree to disagree – but you are missing an excellent opportunity to test your ability to persuade the other side on any issues.

If at least one offer and counter-offer has been sent between counsel, you have already set some important parameters and jump-started the negotiation process. At mediation, you are well on your way to a more productive session, and the first hour is not wasted waiting for you, or other counsel to come up with your first offer.

179

3. Conducts a thorough dress rehearsal

These never go well. They should be painful for everyone. These prep meetings need to be full of realism, pessimism and deflated expectations. Please ensure your client has read everything the other side has sent and fully understands it. I am shocked when I hear counsel say that they are concerned that their client would be "upset" by the tone of the brief or a letter that insults counsel. Last time I checked, litigation was not a musical nor a comedy (although some should be) and your client needs to know that the process can get very nasty, just like those press reviews the day after the play opens. The more they appreciate the dark side of the process, the better they can be prepared to understand what is involved in litigation, and understand the true costs and benefits of settling early.

Taxes payable on wages, EI repayments, credit for mitigation and legal costs should not be new concepts introduced to clients for the first time at the mediation sessions.

Unrealistic case successes must be stated at every available opportunity. Explain again that the numbers in the statement of claim where just "the trailer" to get people excited about the case. Now the real numbers and real first offers must be determined.

I find there is real power in the first number/first offer — just as the opening line of a play sets the scene.

Employers need to be reminded that in Ontario, cause is a difficult hurdle, and older, management level, long-serving employees will make judges swoon. Ask them what they think a jury of the plaintiff's peers would give as an award?

The great new plot twists: human rights damages, moral damages, punitive damages, and the all new fangled ones brilliant plaintiffs' counsel will continue to create and plead, must be reviewed before walking into the mediation. Please discuss whether or not they will be part of the final settlement. In my experience, American and Quebec employers love the way general damages stretch their dollars.

For plaintiffs, please run the numbers before the mediation, to explain what would go to the Canada Revenue Agency and EI after a win in court, and what a mediation settlement could put in your client's pocket "today". I never enjoy doing the fancy math and dealing with the sticker-shock clients suffer when they struggle to understand why the deal on the table is better or equal to a win in court.

Just remember, the worse the dress rehearsal, the better the main performance.

4. Ready for showtime

Show up on time. Latecomers only seated when appropriate! Again, first impressions are lasting impressions.

Are you trying to impress me? The other counsel? The other client? Your client? All are legitimate, but make sure you are making that brilliant soliloquy for the targeted audience. I am neither pro nor anti-openings, just make sure there is a purpose. Please ensure that you meet the players in the room if there are no openings. I find it odd that you would not at least want to eyeball the other client.

I still find it very powerful to hear the client's voice at the table. I also think it gives the other side some insight as to how they would appear at a trial.

5. Brings props

Has your plaintiff client pounded the pavement and Internet seeking new employment? Bring that big thick binder with you. Has your defendant client sent leads and spent just an hour on Workopolis and can prove mitigation is easy? Bring that big thick binder and place it not so gently on the table. Do you have some witness statements to share? Even unsigned, those statements are great to pass around. Please do not send the after acquired "pictures" discovered on the computer post-dismissal. Sometimes leaving some things to our imagination makes for wonderful theatre.

6. Using supporting actors in an appropriate way

Without getting into a diatribe or the psychological concerns, if others, especially parents of plaintiffs are going to be present at the mediation, please deal with their role before the mediation (add it to your dress rehearsal to do list). Not only can they confuse us as to who the client is, it sends a weird message to the defendants. Spouses, friends, and children can be extremely helpful in the process, but you must deal with these shadow negotiators and ensure they know — and you know — what part they are playing. Be ready to move them off-stage and into the "green room" if they are not helpful, or bring them in from the lobby if your client needs the extra support.

Defendants — who is that crackly voice at the other end of the speakerphone? Can I please speak to him or her too? That voice behind the curtain, holding all the authority but not in the room with me is not ideal, but I will work with them if you let me, as I may be able to help you get your message across, or I can help them understand the impasse.

Remember, sometimes the supporting role can be the most out-standing performance and that is why there is a category for them at award shows. The key is not to let them take over if that is not in the script.

7. Uses intermissions in an appropriate manner

You and your client do not have to ask permission to use the washroom facilities but I do love it when you do!

I know our smart phones make it for an easy way to check-in and checkup on all our other business, but in the real theatre, not only are you asked to turn your phones off, you would never, I hope, use the time to answer texts or emails. I need your full attention and I feel awkward disturbing your calls. I also see the look on your client's face when they do not feel they are getting your full attention. Please try to use the time that I am not with you productively. Work on the draft reference letter, contemplate their next number and be ready with your next three moves. Take the time to draft the minutes of settlement, make changes to the release, or redo all the numbers with a general damages component. Let your clients see that today, they are your only focus and that they are really important to you – make them feel like stars!

8. Understand the plot and structure of the whole production

I have seen some clever 30-minute plays, but great theatre needs a little more time. It is interesting how a play and a mediation both need about three hours to complete, including intermissions. Coincidence?

There is a unique ebb and flow to all mediations. Sometimes, you want to race the plot along, but along the way you may lose your audience. Many people want and expect "the dance", often scripted as "they just increased their offer by 10% but we went down by 11%", to be part of the production. You may not like the dance sequence, but if it takes putting on a tutu to get the case settled, I will be happy to help you get into costume. Remember that as a mediator, I am seeing people without their makeup on, behind the scenes, so let me help you deliver some of your most clever lines that gets everyone's attention. We are all editing on the run and reacting to new lines and cues, so if you expect the unexpected and remain positive throughout, the twist in the plot could lead to an even better ending.

Time is money in both businesses. If the show runs overtime, stage crew gets time and a half. Please be respectful that three hours (most employment mediations can be completed in a half-day) goes very quickly so you should be prepared to respond carefully but quickly to all offers.

9. Ready for the encore

The "F word" can often signal the end of the show. However, great productions are always ready for the encore. Please remain open and available to consider another way to wrap up a case that could work. For example, could the plaintiff's counsel bill the defendant directly and include HST? Sometimes, there are little extras that make the performance memorable.

10. Bows with grace and gratitude to fellow actors

Those three hours feel exhausting, often because you have had to spend many hours entertaining your client; it is the play within the play! With minutes of settlement complete, handshakes should follow. If there is no agreement, counsel, please leave the stage knowing that you may be cast together in many more mediations so leave the door open to continued negotiations and organize a plan for the next steps.

"Break a leg!" Oh, that is actually my line for those personal injury lawyers who are now acting in employment cases . . . but that is for another paper at another time!

THE VIEW FROM THE MEDIATOR'S CHAIR

Winning at Mediation

Steve Raymond

I am writing for litigators who are ready to proceed to mediation. Litigators, by their very nature, are programmed to want to win. Everyone enjoys winning more than losing, but finding ways to win in a collaborative exercise can be difficult. I want to examine various aspects of the mediation process and identify key opportunities for "winning" at mediation.

First, there are two main time frames to be considered. The first is the time when you are preparing for the mediation. The second time frame is the mediation itself.

Before the Mediation

Pick the right mediator

This might be the most important step to having a successful mediation, and to achieving an outcome that you and your client will consider a win.

Mediators have different styles and experiences. First, there is the mediator's style. Some mediators are more evaluative of the case than others. Personally, I am quite likely to offer an evaluation of the case at an early stage in the mediation. When you start talking about your case, I will agree with certain points and disagree with others. I will challenge factual assumptions and legal conclusions. I assume that if you chose me, you know this, expect this and want this. But, from time to time, I am again taught the lesson that this is not the case. Sometimes advocates do not want to hear about the weakness in their case or to be challenged in terms of assumptions. In these circumstances, I wonder why have I been chosen? You knew my style.

Second, there is the mediator's experience. Does the mediator specialize in the resolution of employment disputes or is the mediator more of a generalist? Does it matter for this mediation? Is it a highly technical legal dispute in which a good understanding of the law in respect of restrictive covenants matters, or is it more of a personality dispute such that you just need someone who can help the parties get over or past that aspect? Since every mediator will have different experiences and every dispute is different, pick a mediator who is experienced in respect of what you and your client need.

One of the first steps in winning at mediation is picking the mediator who will be best for the matter. When doing so, think about style and experience and keep an open mind to what might be best in each individual circumstance for you and your client.

Now let us review the most important aspect in choosing a mediator. You must choose a mediator you <u>trust</u>. Normally, this will mean a mediator with whom you have worked before, but there might be circumstances where that is not the case. It is always helpful when you need to find a new mediator to choose one based on the recommendation of a colleague. In any event, trust is essential. Trust is vital. Trust is paramount. The best advocates from the very beginning of a mediation treat the mediator as a fellow professional in which they have a high degree of trust. I will explain further as we move to the mediation how vital trust is to winning the mediation!

The Mediation Brief

The other important matter before the mediation is the preparation of the mediation brief. The brief is prepared for many audiences. It is prepared for your client, the other side and the mediator. Think about which audience you most want to influence and how you can do so. Think about making it as user-friendly and understandable as possible. Charts can be a very effective and concise way of providing your point of view. Try to remove irrelevant facts. The most important (and often the most missed aspect) of the brief is that you should tell your client's story. Here is the beginning, here is the middle and here is the end, and, finally, here is why we need to go to mediation! If you think about it long enough, every file can be told like a story. I also find it more compelling, and you want your brief to be compelling, especially when problematic facts are acknowledged and addressed, not ignored. Remember the brief is confidential to the process just like the mediation itself. It is okay to "let down your guard" a little bit and it allows the person reading the story (the brief) to empathize with the situation. I think it is easier in employment matters for plaintiff's counsel, who are almost always representing an individual human being, to do this but the best of the defendant's counsel also make a compelling case. They should make the mediator understand why the organization made the decisions it made and why up until this point it has been unable to resolve the difference with the plaintiff.

THE VIEW FROM THE MEDIATOR'S CHAIR

At the Mediation

What about the joint session?

You need to think about the purpose of the opening statement at the joint session – who is it for? The client? The other party? The mediator? What needs to be communicated? What else might be communicated? I find that all too often the opening statement by the litigator is for his or her own client. Instead, it should be used as an opportunity to persuade the mediator and/or the other side about your client's position in the case. A good opening statement is measured, direct and concise. It should focus not only on the strengths of the case but deal with the weaknesses head on. It might also focus on the reasons why a resolution would be superior to ongoing litigation. I think the best opening statements also indicate that there is a willingness to settle and usually involve some sort of acknowledgement of the position of the other party.

Mediations are stressful for the participants, even before they get going. An opening statement can work to reduce that stress and put the mediation on a strong footing towards resolution. It can also have the opposite effect. I have been involved in too many mediations where one side or the other or both use the opening statement as an opportunity to deliver a "message" to the other side's client. This almost always backfires and puts the success of the mediation at risk from the beginning. More and more, I find that joint sessions are being declined and I do not see any direct correlation between the occurrence of a joint session and the success of the mediation. A good joint session can be very helpful, a bad one very destructive. Often, just moving to the "shuttle diplomacy" can be better.

Trust the mediator at the mediation

This is my most important tip to winning at the mediation. Remember that you chose a mediator that you could trust. Now is the time to put that to work for you and your client. Trust the mediator. As a mediator, I do not care whether the plaintiff gets "five cents" on the dollar, "fifty cents" on the dollar or "one hundred and fifty cents" on the dollar. All I care about is getting to a compromise that both sides can live with. I come in knowing the starting positions of the negotiations. I always ask if there have been any offers made that have not been communicated to me (I find it startling that there so often are!) I then have my "goal posts" for the resolution. Now is the first opportunity to put that trust in the mediator into action. Tell the mediator where you

187

think the deal is. In so many mediations, I wander back and forth between two rooms not knowing what either room really can do or even what they want to do. I am just a participant in a game of "ping pong". Sometimes, I am not even a very active participant, but more of a spectator. Even when I push, probe, ponder, I get little. Often in these cases a resolution is not achieved. I find the advocates who trust me early with an indication of where they think the deal can happen are far more effective for their clients. The sooner I am given an impression (clear or otherwise) of where one side can move I begin to work towards that goal. It does not mean that I can get there — I am not making the decisions in the other room nor in yours — but I have one "target" that I have found and can work with.

The other way in which trust is earned and rewarded is in how and when you speak to your client in front of me. I find it interesting that almost all litigators ask the mediator to leave the room when they want to speak to their clients. Some do not and I find that these litigators win more often. They are demonstrating to me that, first, they have nothing that they need to hide from me (and in many cases they trust me to keep something hidden from the other side as I tell people right at the start of the mediation — I will keep something confidential if you ask me to). Secondly, they are also increasing my confidence in what they say their position is because I do not think that there is some other conversation happening that is different from what I am hearing. Thirdly, they are subtly trying to bring me onto their team. Now the smart litigators know I will never actually be on their team and that I am perfectly prepared to demonstrate in both rooms that I am fighting for you (because I am). But, by letting me hear your conversations with your client, there is no doubt that I am more "bought in" to your position than if I missed the entire conversation and then am brought back into the room to be given the position to take to the other side.

I think it is essential in resolving a difficult matter that the advocates and their clients trust the mediator and demonstrate that trust in him or her throughout the process from the selection of the mediator through the successful resolution of the matter.

Mediation Hints —
A Client Representation Perspective

Mike Silver

The Lawyer's Balancing Act — Adversarial v. Facilitative

A lawyer representing his or her client at a mediation has a dual task. On the one hand counsel are there to ensure that the client gets the best possible result – one which gives effect to the client's interests (which include avoidance of a negative result in court). On the other hand, if a negotiated solution has advantages, counsel must be careful not to be excessively adversarial and indeed he or she is responsible for helping to achieve an atmosphere at the mediation conducive to settlement. This requires a balancing act on the part of counsel which in practice can be difficult to achieve. Counsel has to be comfortable in their own skin and should not attempt to be somebody whom they are not. But this is not a license to let it all hang out either. There must be an intelligent application – in substance and in timing, to one's approach. One has to appraise the nature of the other side (*e.g.*, are they receptive to facilitation), the character of one's own client and their values, the strength of one's case, the style of the mediator, and the time available for mediation, among many factors.

Below are discussions of a few key issues that involve the tussle between adversarial and facilitative styles in counsel representing clients at a mediation.

To Have or Not to Have a Joint Session

I have been mediating full-time for nearly 20 years now and have seen literally thousands of mediations. One manifestation of how lawyers are resolving the balance between adversarial and facilitative approaches is to increasingly dispense with the joint session, on the pretext that it only tends to inflame emotions and heighten resistance to settlement. There is some truth in this belief, although holding too fast to this approach denies the party the opportunity to lay out a convincing argument or to successfully poke holes in the opposing side's case.

As a rule then, should resort be had to a joint session? Does it tend to polarize the parties or drive a wedge into settlement discussions?

In my view it is a very case dependent decision on the part of counsel. As a mediator, I respect counsel's decision on whether to have or not have a joint session. The parties can always be brought back together if there is some reason to do so – such as sharing vital information or to have a question answered face-to-face. In cases where the issues are well understood, and the parties are eager to commence negotiating, the trend is often to skip the joint session.

However, this is and should be the exception to the rule, which is to make submissions so that the other side understands clearly where you are coming from. I have seen many cases where the joint session was dispensed with, only for counsel to find that they have not made their point adequately to the other side. As stated above, the problem can be dealt with by reconvening, but interestingly, I think in all the cases I have mediated where this has happened, I, as mediator, have been the one to suggest and push for getting back together. Counsel are usually reluctant to reconvene and in that sense, if it is helpful to a party to do so, depriving oneself of the initial opportunity to make a submission puts oneself into the position of having to rely on the mediator to know when to reconvene so that you can convey your essential point. Not every mediator will notice the need, or even see it as their role to suggest a re-convening to a party. To some extent then, if you decide to dispense with the joint session, you are to a greater extent placing yourself in the hands/skills of the mediator.

In addition, a joint session can provide an opportunity for counsel to shine and develop arguments that can be persuasive. This "counsel show" can be positive if it impresses one's own client, the other side, and/ or the mediator. It never hurts to be taken seriously!

It is also an opportunity to inject some humour, or to develop some kind of rapport with the other side. Not every joint session submission has to be off-putting! It could provide an opportunity for well placed empathy, or an apology, or a statement of resolve to find a way to settle the case, which is often very encouraging. If one's own client makes a good witness the joint session is the time to demonstrate that by having the client speak. Clients with a genuine understanding of the problem or with genuine feelings are very impressive – and not just to the other side but also to the mediator. A joint session can also be an opportunity for the client to shine and impress the other side.

Finally, a joint session is of course "joint" in the sense that the presentations are mutual. One gets an opportunity to size up the other side and evaluate their arguments and how they come off. Will they impress a judge or jury? Do they appear to be genuine? Are they sympathetic or off-putting? Can they be trusted?

I remember one joint session involving a dog biting case where counsel invited the plaintiff to speak. I asked her just how bad the bite was and she lifted up her blouse to expose scarring over her entire torso! I exclaimed "Wow!", and in separate session the insurer expressed displeasure that I, the neutral, had uttered my remark. The action had a jury notice and I was able to reply that they had seen my gut reaction and how did they really think a jury would react? The case settled quickly!

In another case, a woman who needlessly had had a breast removed (and so subsequently had the other removed so that they could be rebuilt symmetrically) was given the opportunity to speak and in so doing related all her prior negative encounters with Ontario's health system. Her parents' deterioration, her best friend's death, her disabled child's unmet needs — all were tales of stress and woe promulgated by bad experiences with the doctors, hospitals and the whole system. I have no doubt that this presentation influenced the final settlement for general damages as her peculiar interactions were considered as part of her overall psychological suffering.

In short, do not dispense with the joint session lightly. Its utility is sometimes not appreciated at the time it is held. Feel free to get your point across – being "soft on the people but hard on the problem" and give voice to yourself as an advocate and to your client if they are impressive.

The Mediator's Float — Submit or Resist?

One thing a mediator may do after a certain amount of offers and counter-offers, and I do it a lot, is to call counsel and/or the parties together and float a proposal that may have advantages to both sides and may work to settle the case. This has the advantages of speeding up a possible resolution (important when time is limited) and avoiding any reactive devaluation (where the parties invalidate each other's offers, even if reasonable, sometimes for no reason other than that they emanate with the other side).

The proactive mediator has the benefit of having heard each side privately and often develops a sense of what might be a reasonable settlement — reasonable in the sense of rational for the parties and in the sense of being doable. The mediator will often float an idea for settlement that combines concepts previously traded back and forth by the parties in their offers, and which throws both sides a bone. The float may also require each side to move off of previous positions by a calibrated amount, which in itself can be attractive to the parties having to compromise further.

The question is usually asked of counsel, "Can you recommend this to your client?" The best chance for a resolution lies with all counsel recommending the same settlement proposal to their clients. Most clients listen to their lawyers and since the lawyers are the ones who will continue to charge them for their legal work, their advice on when to settle is also practically persuasive.

So when hearing the mediator float, should counsel submit to it, or try to change it or "knock it down a notch" to be more one-sided towards one's own client?

Again there are no rules applicable in all situations. However I have seen lawyers continue to be adversarial at the 11th hour mediator float and then wonder why the case did not settle! Counsel's reaction to the float and their willingness to recommend it can vary. Obviously, many cases end up with the lawyers agreeing with the float and recommending it and the cases settle.

In other instances, counsel may indicate that they cannot recommend the float exactly as is but suggest a tweaking with which they could make an endorsement and those cases often settle. At the other extreme is when the float is provided and counsel indicates that they cannot recommend it or that even if they did their client would never agree. If all parties indicate this then it is a signal to the mediator to shutdown the mediation. A threshold has thus been established which is not doable at the session and accordingly there is not sufficient "settlement DNA" to enable a settlement.

Generally speaking, I find that counsel should be honest about what they can recommend and should not hesitate to attempt some tweaking if it really would make a difference. However, the 11th hour float is **not** the time to get finicky or myopically one-sided. The float is happening because the trading of offers has run its course. The float may be the last best hope to settle the case. If it is going to settle, the other lawyer(s) will also likely be called upon to move so as to maximize the chances for a settlement. All sides must likely "pitch in".

I have seen situations where the parties are willing to move and take the float but one party holds out obstinately. Without commenting on what this does to the relationship between counsel, if there is no good reason for the hold out except that of obtaining some small advantage over the other parties, it can devastate the chances for settlement. For counsel doing this, my warning is be sure you know your client's true intentions and desires. If you are offside and your client really does want to settle, you could have mud on your face. If you are not sure, invite the mediator to have a "fireside chat" with you and your client to sort out the pros and cons and let your client decide.

In one case, neither lawyer thought they could recommend my float but allowed me to put it to their clients without counsel being present. To counsels' amazement both sides took the floated deal! The lawyers involved recognized that their judgment might get in the way of a settlement their clients might want, but they were not sure. They had the courage (and faith in their clients) to step back and let them make up their own minds.

Drafting the Settlement

Many hard fought settlements nearly crumble (or do unravel) at the stage at which they are committed to writing. Perhaps uniquely among mediators, I volunteer to do the drafting because I know I can draft succinctly and by doing so, it is my experience that a lot of the antagonism or knee-jerk rejectionism of counsel or the parties can be avoided. Having said that, if a lawyer wants to do the drafting, I let it happen. The results are not always good. Especially if a laptop is involved, counsel/the parties tend to get very particular about wording and changes. At a minimum, it takes longer to do a draft. In its worst manifestation, counsel keeps thinking of new self-serving things to add and it can derail the deal.

My suggestion is that drafting is not the time to be gratuitously adversarial. Counsel must be diligent to ensure wording that works for the client and above all does no harm. But it is another thing altogether to be reflexively rejectionist or antagonistic.

In my view, there is nothing inappropriate in asking a skilled mediator to draft the minutes. This will remove much potential acrimony, whether induced by "buyer's remorse" or a sense of the other side being too insistent on its own terms in the minutes. Counsel should be present when the mediator is drafting and preferably should address any specific inclusions at that time, as opposed to when the drafting is all finished. If there is something complex or technical to the drafting, counsel should be prepared to collaborate with each other on the wording.

In one case, the settlement provided the defendant to elect option A or option B by an agreed upon date. Option A was much more complicated and required careful drafting. Option B was extremely simple. One of the lawyers had done a draft set of minutes without getting prior approval from the other counsel and the lawyers and the parties got into such extensive bickering that I suggested shelving the more complicated option and simply giving the defendant until the due date to decide whether to settle on the basis of the simpler concept. But the defendant party perked up and said, "No – this option is very important to us", and so we had to make it work. Eventually, with mediator assistance, the right compromise wording was found to the difficulties. It likely would have gone smoother if I had just started drafting and counsel could argue as we drafted, with the mediator playing the role of referee on final wording.

The settlement may be hard won but generally speaking counsel should not upset the apple cart at the late stage of drafting minutes. The fight is over and the goal at this stage should simply be to paper the deal.

CONCLUSION

Mediation of employment disputes has clearly evolved over the last 10 to 15 years. Most employment counsel will find themselves involved in mediation on a very regular basis and they will feel very at ease in the mediation room. However, it is important that each case be looked at individually and that the techniques used are adjusted as needed to take into account the special circumstances of each case and the individual needs of each client. It goes without saying that no two mediations are alike. Differences in the characteristics of the parties, the issues, counsel styles and importantly, mediator styles, will serve to make each mediation unique.

Index

INDEX

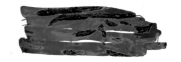

Summer 2018